rob antoun and dan thorp

youth tennis

drills

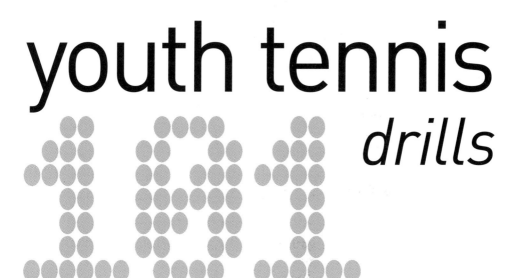

Published in 2010
by A & C Black Publishers Ltd
36 Soho Square
London W1D 3QY
www.acblack.com

ISBN 978 14081 1330 1

A CIP catalogue record for this book is available from the British Library.

Acknowledgements
Cover photograph © Shutterstock
Inside photographs © PA Photos
Illustrations by Mark Silver
Commissioned by Charlotte Croft
Edited by Kate Turvey

This book is produced using paper that is made from wood grown in managed, sustainable forests. It is natural, renewable and recyclable. The logging and manufacturing processes conform to the environmental regulations of the country of origin.

Typeset in 10 on 12pt Din Regular by Margaret Brain, Wisbech

Printed and bound in the UK by Martins the Printers

youth tennis
101
drills

Also available from A & C Black

Know the Game: Tennis
Lawn Tennis Association

Tennis Strokes and Tactics to Improve Your Game
John Littleford and Andrew Magrath

CONTENTS

ABOUT THE AUTHORS

Rob Antoun is a former ATP world-ranked tennis player who has coached at an international level over a 17-year period. He is a PCA-qualified coach and a Tennis Europe and LTA coach education tutor. Rob holds a degree in psychology and is also the author of *Women's Tennis Tactics*.

Dan Thorp is an LTA Registered Professional Coach and is based at Manor Park Club in Malvern. As a coach Dan has a successful track record in many areas ranging from mini tennis to working with national level players, and has also worked as a coach educator for the LTA. In 2006 Dan launched the British Tennis Parents website in collaboration with Judy Murray.

In 2007, Rob and Dan founded Pro Tennis Solutions Ltd – now one of the UK's leading tennis consultancy companies (www.protennissolutions.com). In 2009, they founded www.mytrainingdiary.org – a complete tennis development website for players and coaches of all levels.

ACKNOWLEDGEMENTS

We would like to thank the many players and coaches who we have been privileged to work with over the years – particularly Jane Poynder at Malvern Tennis Academy and Adrian Moll at Maidstone Tennis Academy for their invaluable feedback. We would also like to thank all the coaches who have helped make Pro Tennis Solutions the success it is today.

INTRODUCTION

This book has been written to help coaches, teachers, and group leaders work effectively with junior tennis players of all levels. There are numerous drills and exercises that cover every element of the game, and there is a particular emphasis on how best to work with larger groups.

The book is divided into chapters based on the different areas of play and various stages of the lesson: warming up; coordination and movement; baseline play; net play; serving and returning; doubles; game scenarios; fun games; and warming down. Each drill comes with a simple description, key coaching points to look out for, and suggestions for progressions where relevant.

The best drills in tennis are the ones that encourage players to have fun while learning about themselves and the game. We hope that you find many of these in this book.

Andrew Murray on court in a practice session with his coach, Mike Maclagan.

SESSION GUIDELINES

communication

Good communication is the most important skill that a coach possesses, no matter what level of player they are working with. With young or less experienced players the coach must be a good communicator so that they can explain exercises clearly, control and organise effectively, generate an energetic and positive environment, and motivate players to work hard and to want to improve.

With older and more advanced players the coach will communicate differently, to help players feel positive when they are struggling, give players honest feedback without becoming confrontational, help them to motivate themselves, generate enthusiasm when players are finding it difficult to generate it themselves, and challenge them to work hard and push the boundaries of improvement.

coaching styles

Good coaches use a range of styles to communicate, motivate and instruct their players. Inexperienced coaches tend to have only one style of coaching that they use all of the time. Examples of this would be a coach who constantly asks questions, or a coach who only gives instruction and never gets input from the players.

The most effective coaches are able to sense which style of coaching is most appropriate for the player that they are working with and the situation that they are working in. They are able to adapt their coaching style to suit the needs of the player in any given situation. This is crucial when working with young players because it is often the *way* in which a coach communicates that proves more important than *what* is actually being communicated! Therefore, coaches need to develop their ability to coach using a variety of styles – from directed coaching (giving players instructions on what to do and how to do it) to self-teaching (allowing players to take ownership of their game by finding their own way of achieving effectiveness).

feedback

If players are to learn new skills, or develop an existing skill, they need to be clear about what they are trying to achieve (through the use of goal setting) and they need to receive regular feedback on their progress. Feedback can come from a range of sources: the coach; the player to themselves (e.g. how the stroke 'felt'); from video replay; and from others (e.g. parents). The feedback that the player receives will be based on either the *performance* (i.e. how well the teaching point was executed or how the shot 'felt'), or the *outcome* (i.e. where the ball went). By improving the quality of the feedback that their players receive, coaches can help them to achieve faster and more permanent behaviour change.

For best results, feedback from the coach should be *positive*. It should look forwards to how the shot is going to be better rather than dwell on what went wrong. Feedback should pick out what players have done well – then encourage them to 'add' something extra to their shot rather than correct or replace something that they have just done.

Feedback should also be *well-timed*. Generally, feedback is best given immediately so that players can remember what they have done and will have an opportunity to put it right. It is important, however, not to give feedback after every repetition. Players need to feel that they have had a chance to improve naturally before the coach intervenes. A coach that intervenes too often will frustrate their players, and their feedback will simply turn into 'background noise'.

It is also important to give feedback after 'the good stuff' as well as after an error that is occurring consistently. Sometimes, coaches stop drills to give feedback when the basket of balls has run out, or when time is up, instead of the moment when the performance goal has actually been achieved. This moment is called a 'learning window' and it is crucial not to miss it.

Feedback must also be *specific* and *consistent*. It should relate to the goals agreed by the coach and players at the start of the drill. Coaches should not be sidetracked by too many secondary teaching areas that may arise during a drill. Specific feedback will bring about a much quicker change in behaviour, particularly if it also includes some sort of a measure.

Finally, feedback from the coach needs to be *appropriate* to the players' stage of learning. Since feedback is given based on either the performance or the outcome of a shot (or sequence of shots), coaches need to understand which type is most relevant in each situation. In other words, when players are in the early stages of learning a new skill the feedback from the coach should encourage them to concentrate on the improvements that they are making to the skill, irrespective of the outcome. When players are in the later stages of learning a new skill they will have a pretty good understanding of how they are performing the skill. The feedback, therefore, should now consider the outcome a lot more in order to challenge them further.

demonstrations

The majority of people (and especially children) learn most by watching and trying to copy what they see. Tennis coaches need to use demonstrations on a regular basis in all sessions as a way of giving information as well as feedback to players. It is important to remember that this is a key communication tool that is often under utilised. The basic principles of a good demonstration include:

● Players should be able to see the demonstrations – possibly from a variety of angles

- The level of demonstration should be relevant for the players' tennis level
- The demonstration should be shown several times
- There should be a verbal explanation of the important points to be noted (because some players learn verbally and because different parts of the demonstration will impact on different players – you need to be sure what the important things are that you want them to notice and point them out)
- Children will lack previous experience and will be helped by some verbal cues. They will also need fewer movements to the technique explained to them because they cannot take on board as much information as older players
- Space should be allowed because those players who learn kinesthetically (by feel) may need space to move the racket (although be aware of safety issues with groups)
- The demonstration must relate to the player (e.g. a two-handed backhand demonstration may not help a single-handed player)
- Demonstrations must take place from the correct position on the court
- Demonstrations should be correct tactically and technically – they should be the role model for the actual game of tennis

It is important to realise that it is not always necessary to demonstrate. As players move from the beginner stage to the skilled level of mastering a technique, the value of a demonstration will change. The general principles are as follows:

- At the *cognitive stage* (thinking stage) there should be several and frequent demonstrations of the whole action, so that players understand the movement pattern and can adopt the 'rough' pattern
- At the *associative stage* (practising stage) there is less need for demonstrations as players should have a good understanding of what they are supposed to be doing. A full demo may be needed if they make several mistakes in a row, start to lose confidence and slip back in the learning process. A coach may also use a part demo at this stage as a quick method of reinforcing a particular point
- At the *autonomous stage*, demonstrations are of less value since the action has been learned and players have no need to copy. The coach may choose to demonstrate a small part of the action that is under discussion

awareness of learning styles

When coaches are teaching their pupils a new skill or developing an existing skill they will need to give them information. Coaches need to be aware that learners are able to take on information presented in different forms. The three main forms through which learners are able to take on information are:

- Visually – watching the coach, another pupil, or a role model
- Verbally – listening to an explanation by the coach
- Feel – doing the skill or a related skill practically and learning by how it feels (this is also known as kinesthetic learning)

All learners are able to learn through all three methods, and will usually learn using all of them at the same time. All learners are, however, different as to which is their preferred learning style. Coaches need to be aware that:

- Visual is a very strong learning style for young children
- Elite performers tend to have a stronger preference for kinesthetic learning (feel)
- As children grow and get more experienced their ability to learn through verbal explanation increases

There is often confusion about the implications of the above information. Awareness of the different learning styles will help a coach achieve quicker and more permanent results with their players. The implications for coaches are as follows:

- Coaches should present information to their pupils in a variety of forms. If a coach only presents information in one or two styles (e.g. only through demo and explanation) then they will not be utilising the full range of their pupils' learning abilities
- If a player is struggling to understand and act on information that the coach is giving then the coach should try to present the information in a different form
- Coaches should be aware of their players' learning preferences and perhaps use that style when teaching the most difficult areas
- Coaches should use lots of demos with young children
- With older players and adults, coaches should introduce more explanations so that the learners can understand the reasons behind the teaching

Examples of teaching through visual, verbal and kinesthetic learning are as follows:

Visual
- Demonstrating a particular technique to a player
- Showing a player a video of a role model
- Showing a player a video of themselves

Verbal
- Explaining to a player why it is safer to rally crosscourt
- Asking a player to listen to the sound of the ball brushing across the strings to understand spin

Kinesthetic
- Asking a player to concentrate on a particular muscle group while playing a stroke
- Using existing skills that the player already has (e.g. referring to the skills they have in another sport to help them)

Coaches need to develop their ability to teach using all of the above styles. By combining and varying these styles they will be able to maximise the progress of their players.

session structure

As coaches start to work with players on an ongoing basis their sessions will differ depending on where their pupils are in terms of their stage of learning, the coaching process and proximity to competitions. Coaches, therefore, need to be efficient in running a range of session types. For example:

For teaching a new skill
- Spend time with players discussing goals and the reasons for them
- Demonstrate and explain the new skill
- Used more simple 'closed' practices that allow players to try out the new skill in a non-pressured situation
- Give feedback on a regular basis to keep players on track
- Be very encouraging, yet specific to keep learners positive, yet clear on what they need to do
- Possibly use a more quiet and precise coaching style

For progressing and developing a new technique
- Be very precise and be sure to see the new technique from the first ball hit
- Give players lots of repetition on the new skill
- Start to test the new skill in more challenging situations. Coaches should look to put pressure on the new skill with tougher feeds, until it starts to break down. At that point they should remind the player of the skill and encourage them to maintain it
- Break away from the skill, go and do something else, then come back to it and challenge the player to see if they can reproduce it on the first ball
- Question players to develop their understanding of when they are succeeding in the new skill and when it is breaking down. The coach should challenge players to see if they can fix any breakdowns themselves

Cementing a recently learned technique
- The coach should expect to see the new technique from the first ball hit in the session
- Put players in practice situations that involve lots of repetition on the skill that has been learned
- Motivate players to keep the work rate high
- Occasionally praise players when the new skill is done particularly well
- Get players to repeat any situation where the new skill broke down so that they have a chance to correct it immediately
- Work with players more on the tactical implementation of the new skill rather than the skill itself

Match play
- The coach should challenge players to produce the new skill with quality in the match situation
- Possibly introduce conditions to make sure that the new skill gets used/tested in the match situation

● Occasionally pull players out of the match situation to recreate any situation where the new skill has broken down, so that it can be immediately corrected

working with groups

Tennis is an individual sport played on a fairly large playing area. As such it can be quite a challenge to teach in larger group situations such as schools. However, it is possible, and there are many coaches and teachers who teach tennis very effectively with groups of up to 30 players at a time.

When planning a session for a larger number of players don't think about the number of players first; instead start with the goals for the session. Once these are clear then start to plan the drills that will help the players achieve these goals. Once you are clear on the goals and the types of drills that you want to use, start to think about the number of players you are going to work with.

It is often a good idea to plan as if working with four players first and then expand the lesson plan from there. Think about how you can use all the space available, how to rotate the players and how to adapt the drill to make it work for the situation. For each drill ask yourself the following questions:

How many playing areas do I have?
If you have four courts then that could be eight half-court playing areas. Although, if you have younger players this could be 12 playing areas with three per court.

How many players do I have?
This will always change with a large group, so to a certain extent you can't plan – just get them all going with a warm-up exercise and try to count them!

How many players do I have per playing area?
Divide your number of players by the number of playing areas.

What rotation system will work for this number?
Examples are:
For three players: one player on their own and the other two swap with each other every point
For four players: two players each end swapping every time they make a mistake
For five players: three one end and two the other end swapping every point

The drills in this book are designed mainly with groups of players in mind. Using the process above, coaches and teachers will be able to adapt these drills to fit the exact number of players they are working with.

WARMING UP

Roger Federer warming up and preparing to play on the grass during the Wimbledon Championships.

drill 1 width warm-ups

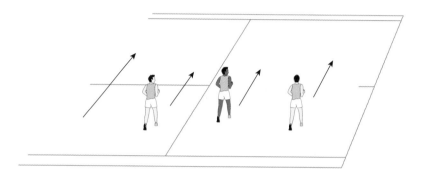

Objective: To warm up the body and to improve all-round agility, balance and coordination.

Equipment: Players on court.

Description: Players line up along the sideline facing across the court. They start by running forwards to the opposite sideline then running backwards back, keeping their head still and balanced at all times. They then progress to using a series of different movements across the court:

(i)   Use a series of side steps across the court and back
(ii) Use a series of crossover steps across the court and back
(iii) Use a series of lunges across the court and back
(iv) Walk with high knees while rotating their upper body across their raised front knee and back

Coaching points: Ensure that players control their movement with good balance and posture and that they take their time getting their movement patterns right – especially when lunging and walking with high knees. Younger children will often want to race each other so work hard at stressing the importance of form over speed.

drill 2   American football

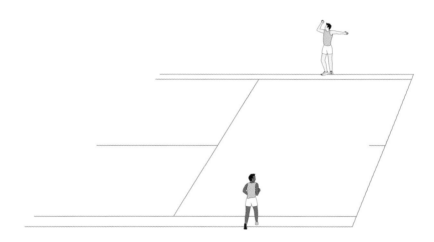

Objective: To warm the body up and to develop coordination and spatial awareness.

Equipment: One tennis ball per team of two players.

Description: Teams of two line up along the sideline facing across the court. Player A runs across the court to the opposite sideline. Upon Player A reaching the sideline Player B throws a tennis ball overarm for Player A to catch. Player A then runs back to Player B and the roles are reversed.

Coaching points: Encourage a strong overarm throwing action with good control of the upper body. Ask the thrower to aim high and point with their non-throwing arm. Look for their shoulders to point diagonally upwards. Encourage the catcher to try to catch the ball above head height whenever possible, since this will help to develop their coordination for tennis. Encourage players to start running quicker across the court as they get warmer.

drill 3 keep the ball moving

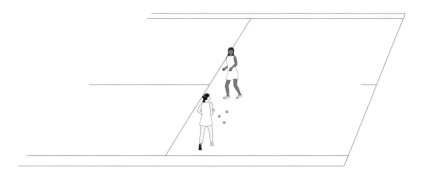

Objective: To warm the body up and to develop coordination, spatial awareness and teamwork.

Equipment: Three tennis balls per team of two players.

Description: Teams of two players work together in an area the size of a service box. On the coach's command, the team has to keep all three balls moving by controlling them with their feet and passing them to each other. The balls must remain in the area at all times. Players do this for 30 seconds and then rest for 30 seconds before starting again.

Coaching points: Encourage players to use small passes with lots of controlled movements in their area. Look for fast footwork and the use of both feet to pass and control the balls. Ask players to communicate well with each other and to maintain awareness of their court area.

drill 4   ready – forwards – back

Objective: To warm the body up and to develop reaction speed and movement skills.

Equipment: Two different coloured balls.

Description: The coach stands on the baseline facing the group of players who are positioned in an alert ready position in lines across the court between the service line and the net. The coach has one ball in each hand. When the coach raises one ball in the air the players move forwards. When the other ball is raised the players move backwards. When both balls are raised the players stop and remain in their ready position.

Coaching points: Encourage players to start in an alert ready position with their feet shoulder width apart and knees slightly flexed. They should keep their head still and their focus directly on the two balls. Look for them to use small, fast feet forwards and backwards. This is a great drill to use with large groups – although make sure players are spaced well enough apart.

Progression: Use different types of signal for a variety of movements. For example, holding a ball to the side means move to the side, etc.

drill 5 shadow strokes

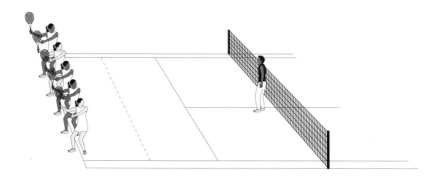

Objective: To warm the body up and to learn about the different strokes in tennis.

Equipment: Players with a racket each.

Description: Up to six players line up across the baseline (if more than six players then players line up across opposite baselines). The coach is positioned in the centre of the court and shouts out the name of a stroke. The players have to move two steps across the baseline before shadowing the stroke. If working with younger players, ask them to make the same noise that their racket should make – e.g. 'swoosh' for a forehand and 'tap' for a volley, etc.

Coaching points: Encourage players to start in an alert ready position with their feet shoulder width apart and knees slightly flexed. They should keep their head still and their focus directly on the coach. Look for the players to take two quick steps across the court, and ensure that they control their racket head when shadowing. This is a great drill to use with large groups – although make sure players are spaced well enough apart.

Progression: Ask players to shadow a series of strokes as if they are playing out a point – starting with a serve or return.

drill 6 — tennis lines shuffle

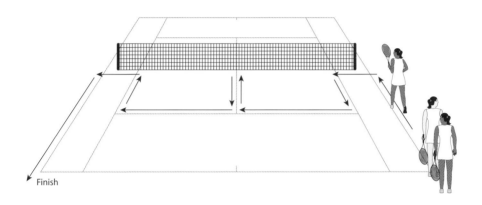

Finish

Objective: To warm the body up, practise stroke technique and learn about the different areas of the court.

Equipment: Players with a racket each.

Description: Players line up behind each other on the corner of the baseline. On the coach's command, Player A runs up the outside tramline to the net, sidesteps across to the inside tramline and runs backwards until reaching the service line. They then sidestep across the service line until reaching the centre line where they run forwards to the net again. On reaching the net the player shadows a forehand volley before running backwards to the service line again. They then continue to sidestep across the service line to the other tramline before running forwards to the net. Upon reaching the net the player shadows a backhand volley, sidesteps across to the furthest tramline and runs backwards to the baseline. Players follow each other but wait for the player in front to start sidestepping across the service line before starting.

Coaching points: Encourage the players to use smooth, balanced movement around the court maintaining control over their body and their racket head as they shadow. Younger children will often want to race each other so make sure quality is emphasised more than speed. Ensure that players remain equally spaced apart throughout the circuit.

drill 7 tramline mirrors

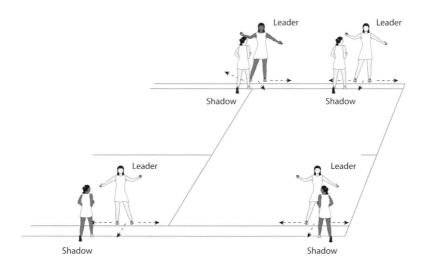

Objective: To warm up the body and to develop reactions with agility.

Equipment: Players in pairs, tennis court lines, one ball per pair.

Description: The players work in pairs and each pair has an area of tramlines to work in. The players stand facing each other – one on the inside tramline and one on the outside. The player who starts with the ball is the 'leader', the other player is the 'shadow'. On 'go' the leader tries to lose the shadow using sidesteps and quick changes in direction while the shadow tries to stay level. Every so often the leader throws the ball to the shadow; when the shadow catches the ball the players switch roles.

Coaching points: Encourage players to use a wide base. This will keep a low centre of gravity and help them to change direction quickly while maintaining good balance.

drill 8 hunt and gather

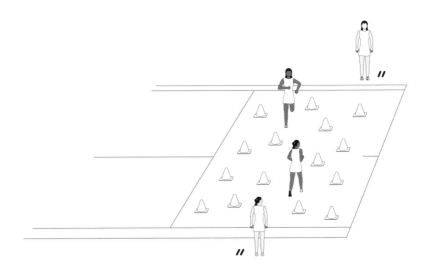

Objective: To develop coordination, speed, teamwork and spatial awareness.

Equipment: Players, 15 marker cones and 5 clothes pegs per half court.

Description: The coach randomly sets down 15 marker cones in the area between the baseline and service line. A peg is placed under five of these cones. Players pair up and compete against another pair – facing each other on opposite tramlines. The object of the game is for each pair to find as many pegs under the cones as possible. Players take it in turns to run and look under a cone before returning to the sideline for their partner to take over. Only one cone can be looked under per go. If a peg is found it should be collected and placed on the pair's side-line. The game finishes when all five pegs have been collected.

Coaching points: Encourage players to move quickly to the cone and pick it up smoothly with their playing hand. If there is a peg underneath look for them to use their other hand to pick it up with, turn the cone back over, and sprint quickly back to their partner on the sideline. This drill is excellent for raising players' spatial awareness and memory since they need to remember which cones have no pegs underneath! Players can help each other choose which cone to look under.

drill 9 ladder warm-ups

Objective: To warm up the body and to develop coordinated footwork.

Equipment: Either a footwork ladder or several line markers/cones.

Description: Set the line markers/cones out in a row about 18 inches apart. Players take it in turns to go through the footwork ladder. Once they've completed the ladder they jog around to the back of the queue. The coach sets the footwork pattern that is to be used through the ladder. Suggested patterns would be:

- Running through – one step in each 'rung'
- Two-footed jumping through
- Double steps in each rung
- Sidestepping – two steps in each rung
- Crossover steps – one step in each rung

Coaching points: Quality is more important than speed, so coaches should emphasise not touching the ladder and maintaining the correct footwork pattern. However, as players get used to the exercise they should try to increase their speed without losing the quality of their movement.

drill 10 team relays

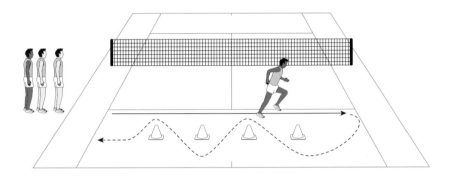

Objective: To develop foot speed, balance and control of movement within a team environment.

Equipment: Four cones per team.

Description: Teams of four line up along the sideline facing across the court. Each team member takes it in turns to run forwards to the opposite sideline as fast as they can and return by zig-zagging through the cones on their way back. The next team member then takes over. Each team member does this three times. The winning team is the first to complete the task.

Coaching points: Ensure that players touch the far sideline with their playing hand and that they push off strongly back into the court with their outside leg. Encourage a fast first two steps across the court, and look for control of the body when moving through the cones.

COORDINATION AND MOVEMENT

Jo-Wilfried Tsonga of France. A great example of how modern tennis players are highly coordinated athletes.

drill 11 throw up and catch

Objective: To develop upper body coordination and good serving technique.

Equipment: One tennis ball per player.

Description: Players spread out and find a space on or around the court area. Each player throws a tennis ball overarm directly above their head as high as possible. They then jump up and try to catch the falling ball above head height whenever possible.

Coaching points: It is important to focus on good throwing technique in this drill. Encourage a diagonal shoulder tilt with the player's front hip pushed out. Look for distance between the player's throwing elbow and back hip, and ask players to point diagonally upwards with their non-throwing arm. Players need to try to combine jumping off the ground with catching the ball above their head since these skills will really help them to develop good serving technique.

drill 12 team throwing targets

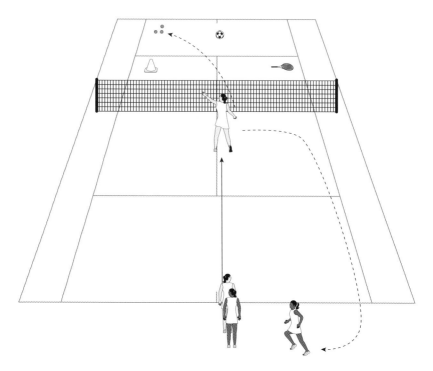

Objective: To develop throwing technique and an ability to judge distance.

Equipment: A basket of balls, court and a variety of targets (e.g. hoops, cones, rackets, bags, etc).

Description: Set out a variety of targets on one side of the court. The players are in teams on the other side of the court, lined up behind the baseline. Each player has a ball. Players take it in turns to go in a relay format. Players bounce their ball up to the net, when they get to the net they throw the ball at one of the targets on the other side. They then run back, the next player starts, and the player gets another ball out of the basket before joining the back of the queue. The winning team is the team that hits the most targets.

Coaching points: Encourage players to aim at a wide variety of targets so they learn how to adapt their throws. Encourage good control while they are bouncing the ball up to the net and then good acceleration and speed when they are running back.

drill 13 turn and catch

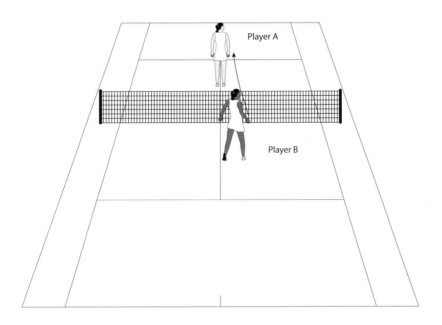

Player A

Player B

Objective: To develop fast reaction skills and upper body coordination to help volley technique.

Equipment: One tennis ball per team of two players.

Description: Working in pairs, players stand two metres inside the service line facing each other over the net. Player A then turns and faces away from Player B. Player B then calls Player A's name and at the same time gently throws a tennis ball for Player A to catch just after they turn around.

Coaching points: The timing of the ball throw is crucial here. Encourage the thrower to 'float' the ball in the air so that the catching player has time to perceive the ball and then move forwards to catch it in front of their body. Look for the catcher to get into an alert ready position and for them to try to catch the ball with either hand – depending on the side that the ball is thrown to.

drill 14 move – catch – lap

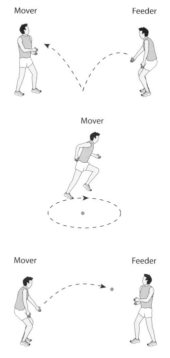

Objective: To develop hand/eye coordination, speed, agility and tennis-specific movement.

Equipment: Players work in pairs on court, one ball per pair.

Description: In pairs, one player is the 'mover' while the other player is the 'feeder'. The feeder starts with the ball and stands facing the mover who is about three metres away in an alert ready position. The feeder throws the ball gently to either side of the mover, the mover moves, catches the ball after one bounce, places the ball on the ground, does a footwork lap around the ball, picks the ball up, throws it back to the feeder, then recovers back to a good ready position. The feeder then throws again. Every six throws the feeder and mover should swap roles.

Coaching points: Ensure that the mover starts in a really good ready position with hands ready, a wide base and an alert attitude. They should get 'behind' the ball to catch and try to never let the ball get behind them. When they do the footwork lap they should use small, fast steps and stay facing the net all the way through.

drill 15 bounce down and catch

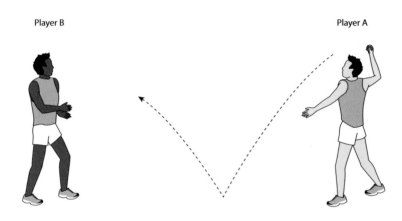

Player B   Player A

Objective: To develop coordination and to introduce an awareness of different ball trajectories.

Equipment: One tennis ball per team of two players.

Description: Working in pairs, players find a space on or around the court area. Player A bounces the ball down to the ground directly in front of Player B. As the ball is bouncing Player A calls 'high', ' middle' or 'low'. Player B has to try to catch the ball at the height specified by Player A. Players switch roles after every catch.

Coaching points: Ensure that players throw the ball hard enough so that it bounces above head height, whilst making sure the ball bounces directly down and up rather than across the court! Look for the thrower to use a relaxed arm and wrist to create a high bounce, and encourage the catcher to jump up off the ground when catching the high bouncing ball.

drill 16 rolling rally

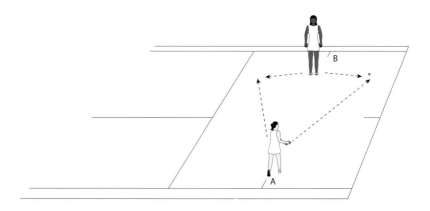

Objective: To develop hand/eye coordination, spatial awareness and effective movement around the court.

Equipment: Players working in pairs on court, one ball per pair, marker cones.

Description: Players work in half courts (width ways across the full court). Use a cone or marker to mark the centre recovery point for each player at the back of the court. The players start opposite each other on their markers; one with a ball and the other in a ready position ready to react to the ball.

The player with the ball rolls it to either side of their partner, the partner moves behind the ball, stops it and rolls it back. The players then continue the rolling rally trying to move each other as much as possible. The players must try to recover in between each roll, back towards their centre marker on the baseline.

Coaching points: Emphasise the importance of a good ready position when waiting for the ball to be rolled. Players should have a wide base and an alert attitude. Encourage players to recover quickly to a good court position after they have rolled the ball, and as they progress discuss how that position is affected by where their roll sends the opponent.

drill 17 throw and catch tennis

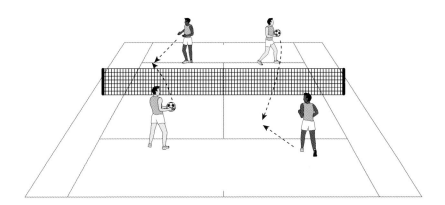

Objective: To develop hand/eye coordination and efficient use of the body when sending and receiving the ball.

Equipment: A football per pair.

Description: Players work in pairs over the net in either half a court or in a full court (if numbers and space allow). Players throw the ball over the net using two-handed throws on either the forehand or the backhand side. Players try to move each other around the court by throwing to the spaces and then recover back to the middle to be ready for the next shot. Players can either work together to build up their highest rally or players can compete and try to win the point.

Coaching points: A priority in this exercise is for the players to judge the flight and bounce of the incoming ball so that they can move efficiently to catch it at a comfortable height to the side of the body. Also, encourage players to use their trunk to rotate when throwing the ball back over the net. Finally, quick recovery back to a good ready position should always be emphasised.

drill 18 goalkeeper games

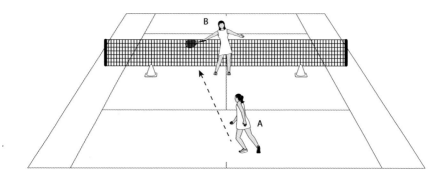

Objective: A fun game to develop hand/eye coordination, movement and racket face control.

Equipment: Tennis court, marker cones, players in pairs with a racket and ball between each pair.

Description: In each pair one player has the racket and is the goalkeeper while the other player has the ball and is the shooter. The goalkeeper stands in a goal that is marked out using marker cones or the lines on the court.

The shooter shoots by rolling the ball to either side of the goalkeeper. The goal-keeper has to make a save by moving to the ball and stopping the ball with the strings of the racket. The shooter quickly recovers the ball, returns to their shooting position and then has another go. The players change roles every 10 shots.

Coaching points: Ensure that the goalkeepers have a good ready position with their racket in the middle enabling them to cover both sides of the goal. Also, remind them to recover quickly back into that position after every save. A more detailed point is to make sure that the goalkeeper is using the forehand and back-hand faces of the racket to stop the rolling ball; this will help them as they progress to play forehands and backhands over the net.

drill 19 fast feet then sprint

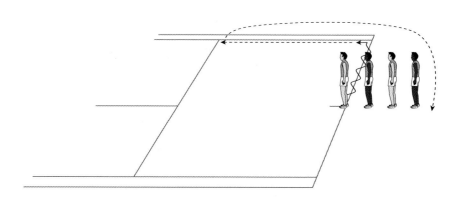

Objective: To improve foot speed and balance.

Equipment: Players on court.

Description: Players line up behind each other at the centre of the baseline. On the coach's command, Player A takes two steps over the baseline then two steps across behind the baseline as fast as possible until reaching the inside tramline. At this point Player A sprints up the tramline until reaching the service line. The next player in line then repeats the exercise. With large groups, organise two teams to race each other along the same baseline. Team 1 moves across to the right tramline whilst Team 2 moves across to the left tramline. Teams 3 and 4 can do the same from the opposite baseline.

Coaching points: Encourage fast, small steps across the baseline and longer, more explosive strides up the tramline – particularly with the first two steps. Make sure players don't lose control of their upper body by keeping their head still and focused forwards. Ask players to start in an alert ready position on the baseline. Allow plenty of rest in between turns (around a 1:4 work-rest ratio).

drill 20 see it, chase it

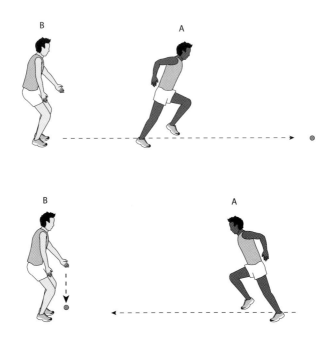

Objective: To develop quick reaction speed, foot speed and coordination.

Equipment: Two tennis balls per team of two players on court.

Description: Player A stands in a ready position on the baseline facing the net. Player B stands behind him/her with two balls in their hand. Player B rolls the first ball through the legs of Player A, who has to chase the ball and pick it up as quickly as possible. Player B then drops the second ball to the side of them. Player A has to turn to chase and catch the second ball after one bounce.

Coaching points: Encourage an alert ready position and a strong drive forwards towards the first ball. Look for the chasing player to turn quickly by using a strong leg drive to push back towards the baseline. Make sure the feeder times the dropping of the second ball well so that the chasing player is challenged appropriately.

drill 21 tramline shadows

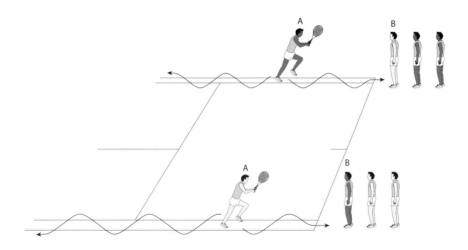

Objective: To develop foot speed, upper body rotation and groundstroke technique.

Equipment: Players with a racket each on court.

Description: Players line up behind each other on the baseline in the middle of the tramlines. On the coach's command, Player A moves forwards from one side of the tramline to the other. As they cross the tramline they shadow alternate double-handed forehands and double-handed backhands until reaching the net. Player B then follows. With large groups, line up four teams using both tramlines on either side of the court.

Coaching points: Encourage fast, light steps starting from an alert ready position. Ask players to sink low (using a balanced knee bend) and drive up through the shadow stroke. It is important for players to really exaggerate the rotation as they shadow the swing.

drill 22 teams to 10

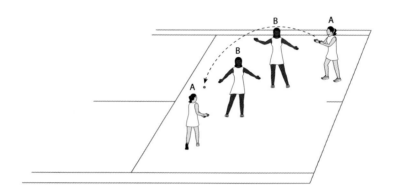

Objective: To develop coordination, movement, spatial awareness and teamwork.

Equipment: Players in pairs on court, and one ball.

Description: Players work in pairs against each other. One pair has to throw and catch a tennis ball to each other 10 times in 30 seconds. Their opponents have to try to intercept the ball after it has been thrown and, if they do, they then try to reach 10 throws and catches. The court boundary for this game is the space between the baseline and the service line and the singles sidelines. Up to four games can be played at any one time on a court since the space between the service line and the net can also be used as a court.

Coaching points: This is an excellent drill to develop hand/eye coordination, movement in and out of space, and teamwork. Encourage good communication between teammates and lots of quick movement and anticipation. Make sure that players stay within the boundaries because this forces them to change direction often and make the most of the limited space available. This drill is also good for doubles partners since it helps them to coordinate their movements and to understand each other more.

drill 23 hitting up

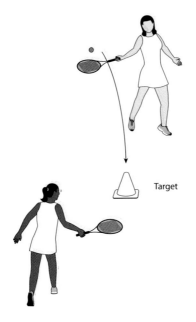

Target

Objective: To develop racket face control and to help players develop a smooth swing.

Equipment: Players work in pairs, rackets, one marker cone per pair and one ball per pair.

Description: Each pair finds a space and places their marker cone on the court. Players take it in turns to hit the ball up in the air, always letting the ball bounce after every hit. If a player can make the ball bounce on the marker cone then they score a point and start a new rally.

Coaching points: Make sure that the players move quickly to get themselves in a good hitting position for each shot. They should aim to be a comfortable distance from the ball for maximum racket face and ball control. Encourage a smooth low to high stroke to hit the ball up as this naturally progresses on to a low to high groundstroke.

Progressions: As players start to find this easier, challenge them to alternate between using the forehand and backhand side of the racket.

BASELINE PLAY

drill 24 tramline tennis

Objective: To get a large group of players rallying and controlling the ball.

Equipment: Players, court, rackets and balls.

Description: The players work in pairs with a racket each and one ball between them. They start facing each other on either side of the tramlines. The players rally trying to land the ball on their partner's tramline – they have to hit the ball up off their racket. If the ball lands on the tramline then the player that hit it scores a point and the rally starts again.

Coaching points: The most important area to concentrate on during this drill is getting the players to position themselves to the side of the ball so that they can then lift the ball up with control. After each shot they need to recover back to a central ready position so that they are ready for the next shot.

drill 25 two-touch rally

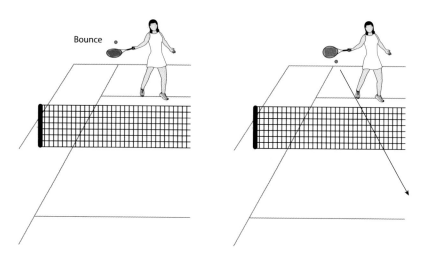

Bounce

Objective: To develop control of the racket head and awareness of a good contact point.

Equipment: Players with a racket each and one ball between a team of two on court.

Description: Players work in pairs rallying over the net within the service boxes. Instead of hitting the ball straight back, Player A controls the ball on the first hit before hitting the ball back with the second hit. Player B then does the same. Further touches can be used if necessary.

Coaching points: Encourage players to get their feet into position early to give them maximum control over the first hit. Ask players to 'cushion' the ball with their strings to absorb the impact and to adjust their feet quickly to get into a good hitting position for the second hit.

Progression: Progress the drill by asking players to control the ball on their forehand side before hitting back on their backhand side – and vice versa whenever possible.

drill 26 throw, hit and catch

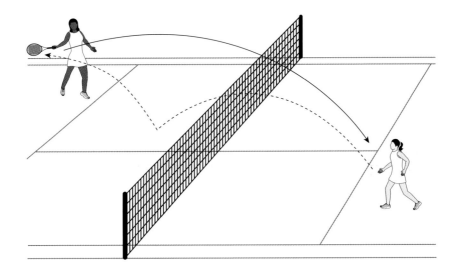

Objective: To develop control and consistency of forehand and backhand groundstrokes.

Equipment: Players, court, rackets and balls.

Description: The players work in pairs and spread out along the net with one player either side. Player A puts their racket down and collects some balls since they are going to be the feeder. Player B has their racket and gets in a ready position a little way back from the net – how far depends on how much they've played before. The feeder throws the balls alternately to the forehand and backhand of the hitter. The hitter tries to control the ball back to the feeder so that they can catch it. Every time the feeder catches four shots the pair switch roles and repeat the exercise.

Coaching points: Teach the players to start in a ready position and to be alert. When the ball is fed to either their forehand or backhand side the important thing is to start their preparation by turning their shoulders towards the ball. The mistake many players make is to prepare by throwing the arm back – this makes the shot very difficult to control.

Progression: Start with a set pattern of alternate forehands and backhands; as the players progress the feeder can mix the feeds up so that the hitter does not know which shot they are going to receive.

drill 27 back, then bounce

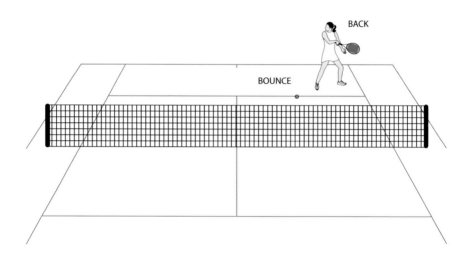

BACK

BOUNCE

Objective: To develop early preparation for the forehand and backhand groundstrokes.

Equipment: Players, court, rackets and balls.

Description: Players rally with each other. The drill can be done with gentle rallying from the service line or longer hitting from the baseline. As the players are preparing to hit the ball they have to say 'back' when they are bringing their racket back and then 'bounce' when the ball bounces in front of them. The timing of the calls need to relate to when they actually do bring their racket back and when the ball actually bounces.

Coaching points: This drill seems simple – but players tend to struggle with it. The key is that they need to be bringing their racket back and saying 'back' before the ball bounces. When they start this drill most players realise that they have actually been bringing their racket back after the ball has bounced – this is too late!

drill 28 hit on the drop

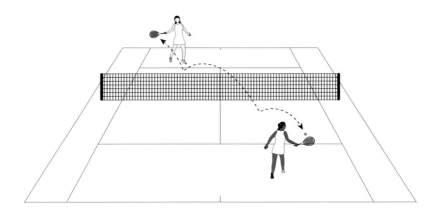

Objective: To maintain a rally by improving court position and a consistent contact point.

Equipment: Players with a racket each and one ball between a team of two on court.

Description: Players work in pairs rallying over the net within the service boxes. Both players must make contact with the ball just as it starts to drop from the peak of its bounce. Players try to maintain a cooperative rally for as long as possible.

Coaching points: Encourage players to try to read the flight path of the oncoming ball as accurately as possible since this will allow for good positioning for their next shot. They should try to have their racket back and ready to swing forwards as the ball bounces on their side of the court.

Progression: Ask players to hit both forehands and backhands within the same rally while still maintaining a consistent contact point with the ball.

drill 29 racing rallies

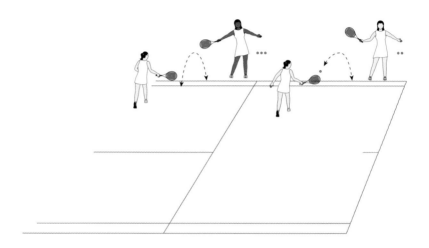

Objective: A fun game that generates lots of activity while improving control of the ball.

Equipment: Players, court, rackets and balls.

Description: The players work in pairs. Each pair has three balls and finds a space over an area of tramline on the court. The players put the three balls well behind one of the players. On 'go' each pair takes one of their three balls and starts to rally across the tramlines. If they get a rally of eight shots then they stop the rally and add the ball to the store of one of the other pairs. It they don't get a rally of eight then they have to keep using the same ball until they do. The winning pair is the one that manages to get rid of their entire ball store and sit down on their tramlines before anyone else.

Coaching points: This is more of a fun game – so there is little need or opportunity to coach. The most important thing is to keep an eye on safety as there is a lot of running around. Make sure that the players running to add a ball on to another ball store do not get too close to a pair that is rallying.

drill 30 collecting tens

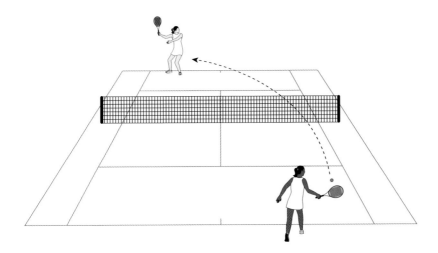

Objective: To develop consistent groundstroke technique and concentration.

Equipment: Players, court, rackets and balls.

Description: Working in pairs and positioned on either baseline, players try to rally 10 shots in a row to each other. Once they reach 10, the players start again and repeat the exercise – trying to achieve as many 10 shot rallies as possible.

Coaching points: Encourage early racket preparation, fast feet around the oncoming ball, and a smooth, controlled swing. Players need to cooperate with each other and try to maintain a consistent ball flight and pace within each rally.

Progression: As players develop, ask them to raise the tempo of the rally by hitting the ball slightly harder, earlier, or with more spin while still trying to reach a rally of 10.

drill 31 21, then switch

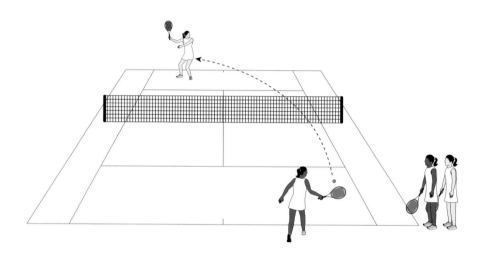

Objective: To develop consistency on groundstrokes with a large group of players.

Equipment: Players, court, rackets and balls.

Description: Players work in groups of three, four or five and each group works in a half court. Each group chooses one player to start on their own at one end of the court, the other players form a queue at the other end with a ball each. The players come in one at a time and rally with the single player. When the rally breaks down the player drops out and the next player comes in to start the next rally. The single player keeps count of how many balls they hit in the court. Once they have reached 21 shots they run down to the other end and the next player takes their turn on their own. See which team can be the first to have all players hit 21 shots.

Coaching points: Help the players to be more consistent on both forehand and backhand groundstrokes by getting them to send the ball with a good 'arc' over the net. To do this they will need to get into a good position so that the ball is arriving to them at just above waist height. Then, as they hit the ball, use a low to high swing – sending the ball back on the same arc.

Progression: If some or all of the players are finding this drill too easy then increase the level of challenge by adding to what they have to do to score a point. For example, the more able players could only score if the ball that they hit lands over the service line.

drill 32 crosscourt rally and recover

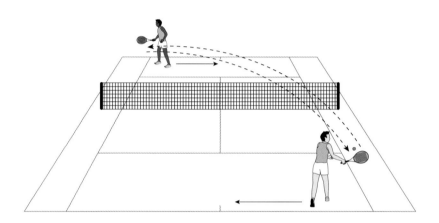

Objective: To develop crosscourt hitting in order to move the opponent around the court.

Equipment: Players, court, rackets, balls and marker cones.

Description: The players work in pairs starting diagonally opposite each other. Two pairs can use the same court. The players start towards the centre of the baseline and feed the ball in crosscourt. The players then try to build a rally on the crosscourt diagonal, however, they are only able to use their 'outside' shot which is the stroke that is nearest the tramline. In order to prevent themselves from having to play their 'inside' shot the players have to recover back towards the centre of the court in between each of their shots. Set rally target totals for the players to work towards based on playing level.

Coaching points: Emphasise the importance of the recovery back towards the middle of the court. Each time they hit the ball the players should recover at least two steps back towards the middle. However, the players should not recover all the way to the middle of the court, as when a shot is hit crosscourt the player should recover slightly short of the centre point to cover the likelihood of a crosscourt reply.

Progression: Once the players have achieved some basic consistency they can progress to playing the point out on the diagonal, again only using their outside shot.

drill 33 cooperate, then compete

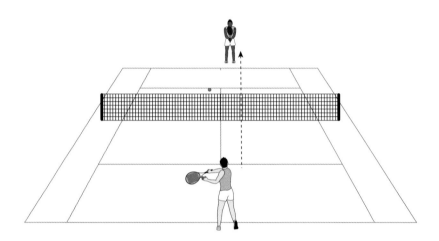

Objective: To develop competitive play while encouraging consistency.

Equipment: Players, court, rackets and balls.

Description: Players play points in either the full or half court depending on numbers and space available. The players have to work together to achieve a consistency target before they are allowed to compete against each other. An example of this would be that the players have to achieve a rally of four – then they can play the point to win. If the players do not achieve the rally of four then neither player scores a point and they have to try again.

Coaching points: Players should be developing spin on their forehand and backhand groundstrokes to do this drill well since it will help them achieve the balance needed between consistency and aggression. Encourage them to accelerate the racket from low to high through the stroke, but to lead with the top edge of the racket on the follow through. This will brush the racket face across the ball and generate spin.

Progression: Either progress to higher targets or make the target more specific. For example, the challenge could remain a rally of four, but all shots have to be backhands.

drill 34 hit with flight

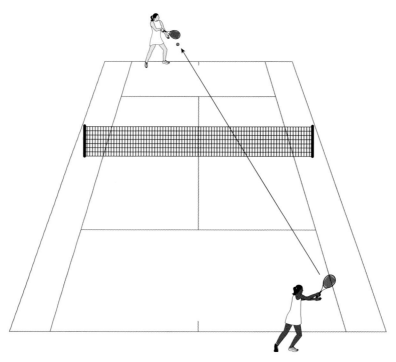

Objective: To learn how to keep an opponent behind the baseline when rallying.

Equipment: Players, court, rackets and balls.

Description: Players rally crosscourt to each other with the aim of keeping their partner playing from behind the baseline. Players score +1 every time their partner hits from behind the baseline and –1 every time their partner hits from inside the baseline. The first player who gets to +10 wins the game. If there are more than four players on a court, keep a cumulative team score and rotate players around after two rallies to ensure all players play with a number of different partners.

Coaching points: Groundstroke depth can either be achieved by hitting the ball deeper into the court using the same ball flight, or by hitting the ball with more topspin so it bounces higher and deeper than normal. Encourage players to choose one of these options with the aim of getting the ball to rise as it crosses the baseline after bouncing in the court. Generally, players will need faster racket head speed and a stronger ball strike to achieve this.

Progression: Progress to allowing a player to approach the net and play the point out if they have forced a short ball from their partner. Play the point out crosscourt (including the tramlines) in this situation.

drill 35 switching drill

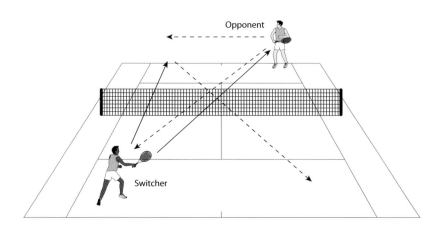

Objective: To develop the ability to change the direction of the ball in a baseline rally.

Equipment: Players, court, rackets and balls.

Description: Two players rally crosscourt with one of the players being designated as the 'switcher'. When a shorter crosscourt ball is hit to the switcher (e.g. a ball that lands inside the service box), the switcher is allowed to hit the ball down the line instead of crosscourt. The switcher's opponent has to defend against this shot by moving across the baseline and hitting crosscourt again. A crosscourt rally from the opposite diagonal continues until the switcher changes direction again.

Coaching points: Make sure the switcher chooses an appropriate ball to change direction with and encourage a large margin for error on this shot (since it is being hit down the line into a smaller space). Encourage the switcher's opponent to defend by hitting a high, deep ball back crosscourt after the switch shot. Stress how effective a series of good switch shots are by noting the defensive position of the switcher's opponent.

Progression: Progress to allowing the players to play the point out in the whole court once the switch shot has been played. If the switcher holds too much of an advantage, allow the switcher's opponent two points for every one point the switcher wins. Play points to seven before switching roles.

drill 36 depth accumulator

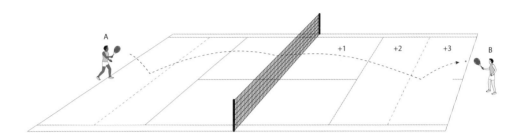

Objective: To develop consistency and depth of groundstrokes.

Equipment: Players, court, rackets, balls and six court lines.

Description: Using court lines make a 'depth line' between the service line and baseline across the court. Each player takes it in turns to rally for one minute – trying to hit as deep as possible into the court. The player scores +1 if the ball lands in the service box, +2 if the ball lands between the service line and the depth line, and +3 if the ball lands between the depth line and the baseline. The player's partner calls the score after every point that is scored and tries to help the player by rallying as cooperatively as possible. Two rallies can be scored at the same time when the players rally down the line into one half of the court. With six players, use the third player in each group to call the score.

Coaching points: Players need to find a rhythm when trying to hit the ball deeply. Encourage a higher ball flight and make sure the players don't simply 'push' the ball in just to score points. Look for early preparation of the racket and a consistent contact point in front of the body.

Progression: Coaches can use this drill as a session starter to help focus their players' minds immediately. It can also be used as a way of monitoring progress – for example, keep scores on a regular basis and note the improvement in each player's score as the term progresses.

drill 37 defend, rally, attack!

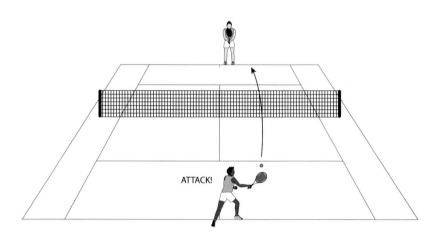

ATTACK!

Objective: To develop an understanding of shot selection.

Equipment: Players, court, rackets and balls.

Description: Players rally in pairs ideally in a full singles court, although the drill will work in a half-court track if there are more players. The players play points, but while playing the point the players have to call 'defend', 'rally', or 'attack' for each shot that they hit. The call should reflect their tactical intention on the shot that they are about to play.

Coaching points: The drill is about recognising the incoming ball and making the right decision about the shot they are going to hit, so calling early is crucial since it shows that the player is making early decisions. Discuss with the players the decisions that they make and how that decision affects the stroke that they hit. Players who do this well will adjust the ball flight and pace of the ball that they hit based on the decision that they make.

drill 38 constructor vs. defender

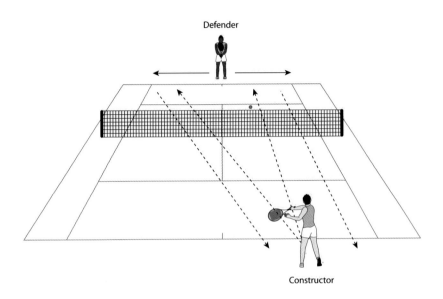

Defender

Constructor

Objective: To learn how to pressurise an opponent by using consistency and accuracy.

Equipment: Players, court, rackets and balls.

Description: The 'constructor' is positioned on one half of the baseline and rallies to alternate sides of the court (i.e. crosscourt then down the line). The 'defender' has to defend against these shots by moving across the baseline and hitting back to the constructor throughout the rally. Play the point out using this pattern and score first to 10 – with the defender scoring two points to every one of the constructor. Switch roles after each game.

Coaching points: The objective of this drill is for the constructor to consistently pressurise the defender and to win the point through a sequence of shots – rather than trying to hit one big winner! It is important to encourage players to build an advantage in the rally through consistency and accuracy. The defender's role is to try to frustrate the constructor into making an error by defending with good depth, variety and determination.

Progression: As competency increases, allow the point to be played out in the whole court after the constructor hits three alternate shots. This should be enough to build an advantage, but it also allows the defender the chance to play in the open court if defending effectively enough.

5

NET PLAY

Grigor Dimitrov from Bulgaria, one of the rising stars of men's tennis, hits a high backhand volley to finish a point from the net.

drill 39 volley hands

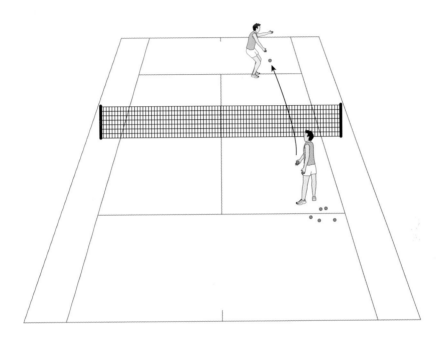

Objective: To develop the basics of volley technique with beginners.

Equipment: Players, court, rackets and balls.

Description: The players work in pairs over the net. One player is the feeder – they collect a store of balls to throw to the hitter. The hitter stands in a ready position on the other side of the net, but without a racket. The feeder throws the balls to the hitter's forehand and backhand side, the hitter goes to the ball and blocks it with the palm of their hand for a forehand, and with the back of their hand for a backhand. After each block the player should recover back into a good ready position. After five volleys on each side the two players switch roles.

Coaching points: The most important thing is that the player should not swing their hand at the ball; they should just block it so that the ball drops down in front of them. A further point is that the fingertips should be pointing up slightly as the player blocks – this replicates the correct volley position.

Progression: As players get the hang of the action required the racket can be introduced. Encourage the players to use the correct continental grip and to continue with the blocking action so that the ball remains under control at all times.

drill 40 make a wall to stop the ball

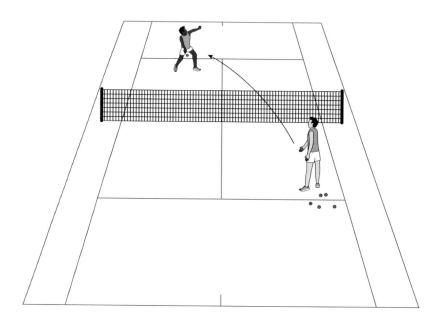

Objective: To help players develop good volley technique and movement at the net.

Equipment: Players, court and balls.

Description: The volleyer stands two metres from the net in an alert ready position but without a racket, and their partner faces them across the net with a handful of balls. The partner throws a ball to the volleyer underarm. The volleyer moves forwards to 'volley' back the ball with the palm of their hand before moving back to a ready position. The volleyer uses either hand depending on which side of them the ball is thrown to. Repeat 10 times before switching roles.

Coaching points: Encourage a strong hand on contact with the ball using a firm wrist and with fingers facing upwards. Make sure players move forwards to meet the ball and that they recover to their original ready position after each volley.

Progression: As players progress, ask the feeder to mix up the feeds in terms of direction and height. Look for the volleyer to use the same firm wrist even if the ball is above shoulder height or below knee height.

drill 41 volley and catch

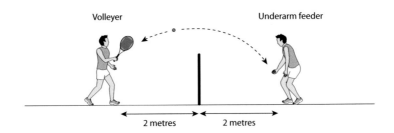

Volleyer   Underarm feeder

2 metres   2 metres

Objective: To develop control of the racket face and 'feel' for the ball when volleying.

Equipment: Players, court, rackets and balls.

Description: The volleyer stands two metres from the net in an alert ready position and their partner faces them across the net with a handful of balls. The partner throws a ball to the volleyer underarm. The volleyer moves forwards to volley the ball back to the feeder. The feeder tries to catch the ball without letting it bounce. Repeat the exercise for the forehand and backhand volley before switching roles.

Coaching points: Encourage the use of a firm wrist on contact with the ball and look for players to volley the ball softly to allow the feeder to catch the ball. This will also help the volleyer to develop a 'feel' for the volley. Make sure the volleyer moves forwards to meet the ball and that they recover to their original ready position after each volley. Look for the feeder to throw the ball cooperatively at around waist height for the volleyer.

drill 42 wall volleys

Objective: To develop sound volley technique and improve fast reactions at the net.

Equipment: A wall, players with rackets and balls.

Description: Players work on their own using a section of wall (without windows!). Players stand about two metres away from the wall and either throw or hit the ball against the wall to start the rally. The players then have to build a rally against the wall; however the ball must not bounce at any time. Players try to get the highest rally on forehand and backhand volleys.

Coaching points: Ensure that the players have their racket heads higher than their wrists; this will help to maintain the correct volley position. If their racket heads drop then they will maintain the rally using the incorrect technique.

Progression: Challenge the players further by: asking them to alternate between forehand and backhands, stepping further away from the wall, increasing the pace of the rally.

drill 43 volley rally

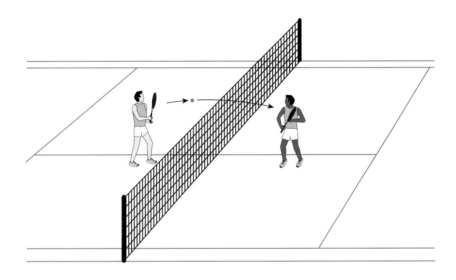

Objective: To develop fast reaction skills and consistent control of the racket face when volleying.

Equipment: Players, court, rackets and balls.

Description: Players volley to each other from inside the service box and try to reach a rally of 10. The ball is not allowed to bounce and volleys should be hit from both the forehand and backhand sides. The pair tries to achieve as many rallies to 10 as possible.

Coaching points: Encourage players to use a firm wrist on contact with the ball with a contact point in front of the body. Players need to use a small split-step in between volleys in order to maintain their balance for the next shot. Encourage cooperation and positive feedback.

Progression: During the volley rally either player can choose to play a lob volley (a volley hit over the head of the player's partner). As soon as this shot is hit the point is played out competitively in the full court (if two players per court) or in the half court (if four players per court). Encourage players to make smart decisions as to when to hit the lob volley, for example, by hitting the lob volley when the player's partner is very close to the net.

drill 44 low to deep – high to angle

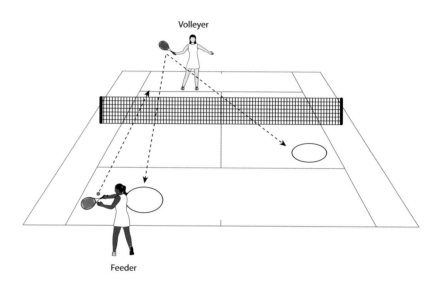

Volleyer

Feeder

Objective: To develop sound decision making and strong technique on low and high volleys.

Equipment: Players, court, rackets, balls and hoops for targets.

Description: Players work in pairs with one player positioned at the net and the other on the baseline. Place a deep hoop target between the service line and the baseline, and a short-angle hoop target inside the service line and just inside the singles sideline. The baseline player feeds either a high or low ball to the volleyer at the net. If the ball is low, then the volleyer must try to hit the volley into the deep target, if the ball is high then the volleyer must try to hit the volley into the short-angle target. Set a target of 10 volleys to be hit before the players switch roles.

Coaching points: This is an important drill because it teaches players the best area of the court to volley to depending upon the difficulty of the shot. If the volley is low and the net player is under pressure, the best area to hit to is deep down the middle of the court. This volley will often prevent the baseline player from attacking and reduces the angles available for their next passing shot. If the volley is high and the net player is in command of the rally, the best area to hit to is short and wide of the baseline (i.e. a short-angle volley). This volley forces the baseline player to move a great distance in a short space of time and 'pulls' them off the court – leaving a big space for the net player's next shot.

Progression: Introduce a two-ball pattern where the first volley is hit deep down the middle and the second volley is hit short and wide.

drill 45 1–2 volley – play

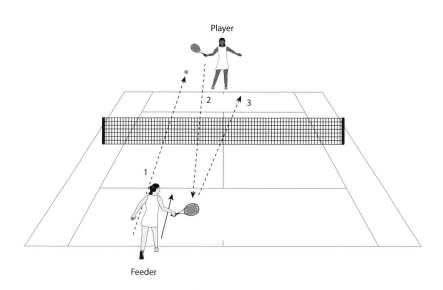

Player

2   3

1

Feeder

Objective: A competitive game that builds consistency on the first volley.

Equipment: Players, court, rackets and balls.

Description: Players work in pairs either on a half-court track or on the full court. Both players start on the baseline. The players have to build a rally of three shots before they play the point to win. The three shots have to be a feed from the baseline, a groundstroke reply, and a volley – then the players play to win with one player at the net and the other at the baseline. The important point is that the player who feeds the ball in has to move in to the net immediately so that they are able to volley the third ball of the rally.

If a rally of three shots is not achieved then no point is scored and the players have to try again to get the rally of three. Once the players have achieved this and scored a point then they repeat the exercise with the other player starting the rally.

Coaching points: The player that feeds the ball in must 'follow their feed'; they need to be quick getting forwards. They then need to steady themselves using a 'split-step' as their partner is hitting the ball back. This way they can be balanced for the volley.

drill 46 volley 11

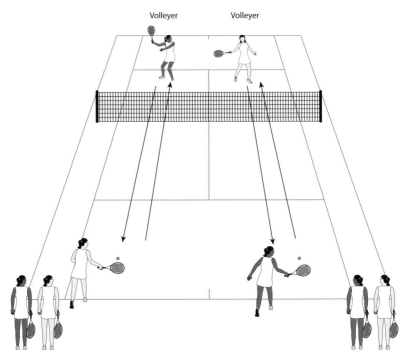

Volleyer   Volleyer

Objective: To develop volley consistency.

Equipment: Players, court, rackets and balls.

Description: Players work in a half-court track in a group of three, four or five depending on numbers. In the group, one player starts on their own as the single player and is positioned at the net. The other players take it in turns to come in and start a rally from the baseline against the net player. Every time the rally breaks down the baseline player drops out and the next player comes in. The net player counts how many volleys they get into the court. Once they have got 11 volleys into the court they move to the other side of the net and the next of the baseline players takes their turn as the single net player.

Coaching points: Make sure that the net player is starting in a good ready position and is recovering back into that position between each of their volleys. Help them further with their consistency by getting them to meet the ball in front of them, but with a blocking action rather than a swing.

Progression: Make the drill tougher by specifying that the volley only scores if it lands beyond the service line or into a particular target area.

drill 47 net play champions

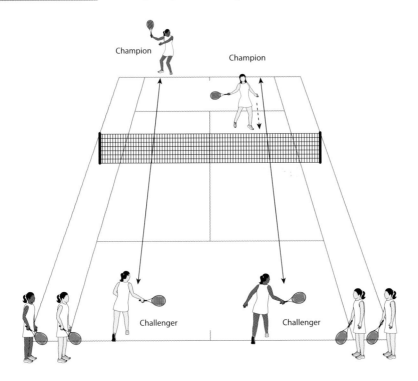

Objective: A competitive game that encourages positive net play.

Equipment: Players, court, rackets and balls.

Description: Players work in groups of three, four, or five and play either in a full court or a half-court track. One player plays on their own at one end of the court – they are the 'champion'. The remaining players take it in turns to come in, feed the ball in, and then play the point out against the single player. To replace the champion the challenging players have to win a total of three points. However, if they win a point from the net then they win three points automatically and become the champion straight away. When there is a new champion all the challenging players return to zero points.

Coaching points: Encourage the challenging players to approach the net to try to win three points straight away. However, help them to understand that they do need to choose the right time to go in. They should wait for a short ball from their opponent to allow them to get closer to the net to play their approach shot.

Progression: Add the condition that if the champion hits a winning passing shot or lob then they send their opponent back to zero points. This makes the challenging players more selective about which shots they come to the net on.

drill 48 net play patterns

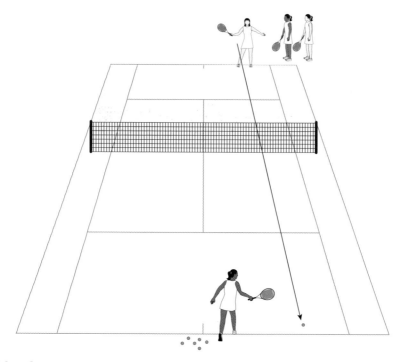

Objective: To develop good volley technique and a sequence of net play shots.

Equipment: Players, court, rackets and the coach with a basket of balls.

Description: Player A lines up just inside the centre of the baseline and faces the coach who is in a similar position on the other side of the net. The other players line up behind Player A waiting for their turn. The coach feeds a short ball for Player A to hit an approach shot with. The approach shot should be hit down the line. The coach then feeds a second ball which Player A volleys, a third ball (a lob) which Player A smashes and a final ball which Player A volleys again. After playing this four-shot sequence Player A runs around the other side of the court to collect the four balls which are put back in the coach's basket and then returns to the waiting area.

Coaching points: Try to feed each ball from a relevant court position. This means moving close to where the player hit their previous shot to, so the direction of the next feed remains realistic. Also, look to feed the next ball based upon the quality of the player's previous shot. For example, if the player hits an excellent smash then you should feed an easy fourth ball for them to volley for a winner.

Progression: Progress this drill by playing the point out with the player after the smash has been hit.

drill 49 approach points

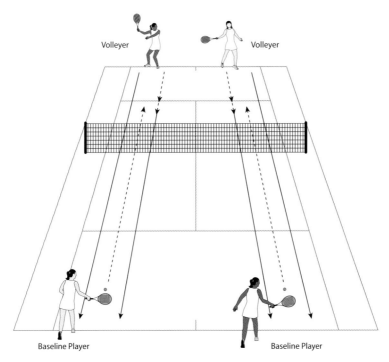

Volleyer · Volleyer

Baseline Player · Baseline Player

Objective: A high-energy game that develops confidence in approaching the net.

Equipment: Players, court, rackets and balls.

Description: The players work in half-court tracks. They play against each other in pairs, although the drills will also work with more players rotating around. Both players start on the baseline, one player feeds the ball in to start the point. The player who feeds the ball in has to follow their feed in to the net and try to win with volleys and smashes. This player has to get in front of the service line before the ball gets back to them otherwise they lose the point straight away. The players take it in turns to feed the ball in, so that all players get an even number of turns at the net.

Coaching points: As a player moves to the net their first volley is often the toughest since they have to play it further away from the net. The key teaching points for first volleys are:

- To balance before the volley with a split-step as the opponent hits the ball
- To get to low volleys by bending the knees rather than by dropping the racket head
- To move forwards after the first volley, following the line that they have just hit.

drill 50 position to smash

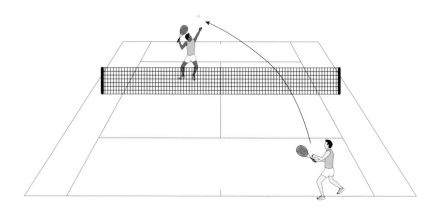

Objective: To develop accurate positioning for the smash.

Equipment: Players, court, rackets and balls.

Description: Players work in pairs with one player at the net and one player at the baseline. The net player is practising positioning for the smash and the baseline player is the feeder. The feeder lobs the ball up into the air – as if they were trying to get the ball over the net player's head. The net player has to turn sideways and position for the smash. Once they are in position instead of hitting the smash they catch the ball in their spare hand with their arm outstretched. Once the net player has caught five balls then the players switch roles.

Coaching points: The important point the players need to grasp is to turn sideways before they start to move for the smash – once they do this they will move more easily. The players should bring their non-hitting arm into the air as they move back for the smash – this will help them to sight the ball in the air and make a cleaner contact.

drill 51 feeding smashes

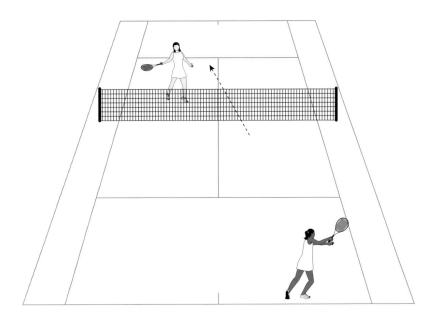

Objective: To help develop effective lobbing technique against an opponent at the net.

Equipment: Players, court, rackets and balls.

Description: Players work in pairs in a half-court track. One player starts at the net with the other player on the baseline. The baseline player starts the drill by feeding the ball in for the net player to volley. Once the volley has been played the point is played out, but the baseline player can only use the lob for the rest of the point. The players play first to five points – at which point the players switch roles and play a new match. If the net player starts waiting for the lob by 'hanging back' behind the service line then the baseline player is allowed to hit a passing shot instead. However, whenever the net player is positioned inside the service line then a lob must be hit.

Coaching points: Encourage the baseline player to hit the lob with plenty of height and depth. If an error is made, it is much better for the lob to be hit too long than too short since a short lob will often be smashed for a winner – allowing the net player to gain valuable confidence! For more advanced players, encourage both the blocked lob and the topspin lob to be hit within the same point. This will enhance a player's feel and control of the racket head.

Progression: Set a rule that the baseline player's first two shots must be lobs but then allow any shot to be played after this.

drill 52 volley then smash

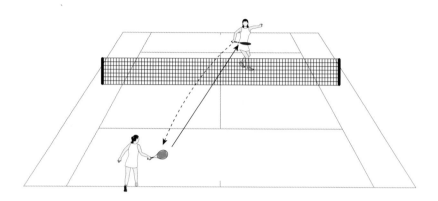

Objective: A competitive game to test movement back to the smash.

Equipment: Players, court, rackets and balls.

Description: Players work in pairs in a half-court track. One player starts at the net with the other player on the baseline. The baseline player starts the point off by feeding the ball in for the net player to volley. The net player volleys the ball in and the baseline player tries to beat the net player with a lob – after this the players play the point to win using any type of shot. The players play first to five points – at which time the players switch roles and play a new match.

Coaching points: Make sure that the net player does not start to move back until the lob is hit, even though they know that the lob is coming. This way they will have to practise the correct movement. Once a net player has hit a smash they must recover quickly back up to the net so that they can take advantage of any weak replies and put the ball away with an angled volley.

SERVING AND RETURNING

At 6 foot 5 inches tall, Marin Cilic of Croatia is one of the most powerful and effective servers in the men's game.

drill 53 serving golf

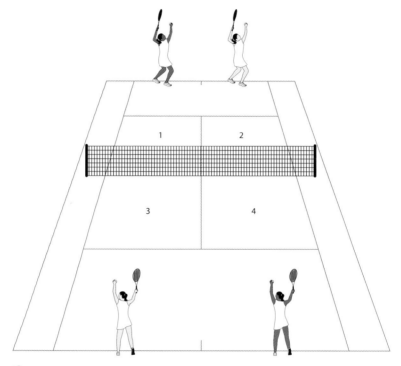

Objective: A fun, active game to develop players' serving consistency.

Equipment: Players, court, rackets and balls.

Description: The aim of the drill is to hit a serve into every service box on the courts available. The number of serves required will depend on how many courts are being used; for example, two courts would be eight service boxes – so that would be eight holes to complete the round of service golf. Players count how many serves it takes them to complete the serving course. The player with the lowest score is the winner.

Coaching points: Emphasise the importance of a consistent ball placement for consistent serving. The main areas to help players with this are: a balanced starting position with both hands relaxed and together; a smooth start to the motion without excess movement; and a consistent placement of the ball using a straight arm.

Progression: It is always best to avoid serving in the net. As a rule, it is better to serve the ball too long than in the net. Encourage this by making the net 'out of bounds'. If a player serves in the net then they have to add two shots on to their score.

drill 54 serving stepping stones

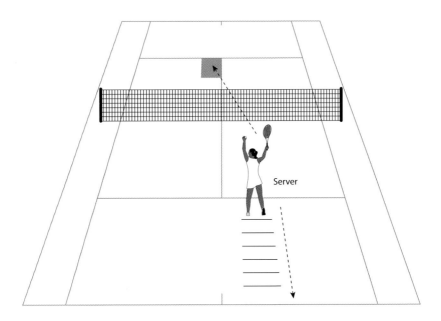

Objective: To develop players' confidence and consistency when serving.

Equipment: Players, court, rackets and balls.

Description: Players start on the service line and aim to serve into the diagonal service box. Every time they get a serve into the court they take a step back before serving again. The players have to try and work their way back to the baseline. Once they've got three serves in from the baseline then they've finished the task. This can be organised as a race, although quality can suffer if it is done this way.

Coaching points: Make sure that players concentrate on an accurate and consistent set-up routine before every serve - especially as players are moving back in between serves. Their routine should always start with positioning the feet before the hands and racket are set up. Be aware of safety in this drill and ensure that players are not serving at other players serving back the same way.

Progression: Make the drill more challenging by setting target areas within each service box that need to be hit before moving back. Getting players to work on direction from closer in is an excellent way to improve their racket face control.

drill 55 serving on balance

Objective: To develop coordination and balance of the body when serving.

Equipment: Players, court, rackets and balls.

Description: Players line up to serve behind the baseline as normal, however, they are not allowed to move their feet at any time throughout the serving process. They are allowed to lift their heel off the ground as they hit the ball and follow through, yet their toes must stay in contact with the ground!

Coaching points: This is an excellent drill to help players align and balance their body more when serving. When attempting this for the first time it is usual for players to lose their balance. However, as they get used to their feet being restricted, they often find that their ball toss becomes straighter (it has to in order to prevent them losing balance) and their body uses only the necessary movements for them to execute the serve. This drill will rapidly develop a player's serve technique.

drill 56 pick up and throw

Objective: To develop the body coordination required to serve more effectively.

Equipment: Players with one tennis ball each.

Description: Players line up across the baseline and set up as if they are about to serve (without a racket) with a tennis ball placed just by the outside of their back foot. The player rocks back as if starting the service motion, but then bends to pick the ball up off the ground with their throwing hand before throwing it over the net.

Coaching points: When setting up to serve, make sure the player's feet are shoulder width apart, their arms are relaxed, and their hands are together and forwards. Encourage a balanced weight transfer onto the back foot as the ball is picked up, and then forwards as the ball is thrown. Look for the throwing action to be as smooth as possible, with the throwing shoulder starting below the height of the non-throwing shoulder (this will help the player throw the ball upwards as well as forwards).

drill 57 two-ball serve shadow

Objective: To improve coordination, rhythm and balance when serving.

Equipment: Players with two tennis balls each.

Description: Players line up across the baseline and set up as if they are about to serve,without a racket but with a tennis ball in each hand. The player starts the service motion and places the ball in the air with their non-hitting hand as normal. They then throw the ball in their hitting hand up and against the ball that is already in the air. The aim is to try to hit the first ball with the second by using a smooth and balanced throwing action.

Coaching points: When setting up to serve, make sure the player's feet are shoulder width apart, their arms are relaxed, and their hands are together and forwards. It is important for the ball toss and the throwing action to coordinate, so encourage smooth, relaxed, coordinated movements of the arms. Look for the player to throw the second ball upwards as well as forwards.

drill 58 bounce then serve

4   3   2   1

Objective: To help players get used to serving with the correct serving grip.

Equipment: Players, court, rackets and balls.

Description: Players line up on the baseline ready to serve. Using the correct serving grip (continental grip is recommended), the player bounces the ball to the ground three times in a row using the hitting side of their racket. Immediately after the third bounce the player catches the ball in their non-hitting hand and goes into their usual service motion. The aim of the drill is for the player to have kept their service grip throughout the service action.

Coaching points: Encourage players to 'pronate' their wrist when bouncing the ball to the ground (i.e. keeping their strings perpendicular to the ground) – this will help them to keep their strings facing the intended target when serving. Spreading the fingers up the grip slightly will help increase 'feel' for the ball and will also relax the arm. Check that the serving grip has been used by looking at the grip after the serve has been hit.

Progression: As players get used to the grip, reduce the number of bounces from three to two to one. Then ask players to serve without bouncing the ball and get them to check their grip after each serve.

drill 59 serving targets

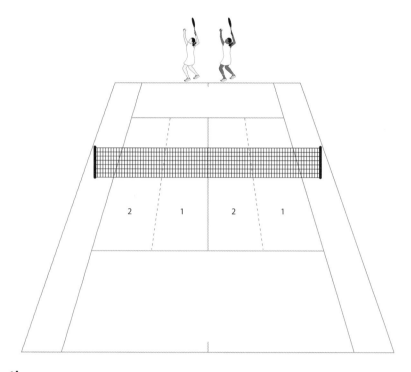

Objective: To develop players' ability to direct the serve to specific targets.

Equipment: Players, court, rackets, balls and marker cones.

Description: Mark out target areas in the service boxes using the cones. The target areas can be changed depending on the level of the players. The best target to set if the players are new to the drill is to split the service box into two halves. The players can then practise directing the serve to either side of the box. Discuss with the players which is likely to be the returner's forehand and backhand so that they can think about which might be the best tactical choice.

Coaching points: Ideally players should have the same set-up for every serve no matter where they are aiming the ball, since this prevents their opponent from reading its direction. Players should direct the ball on contact using only slight adjustments of the racket face. This way the set up and ball placement can be the same for every serve.

Progression: As players progress, develop the target areas set. Challenge the players more by setting two target areas in each box – one for the serve down the middle and the other for the serve out wide.

drill 60 serve – return – 3 then play

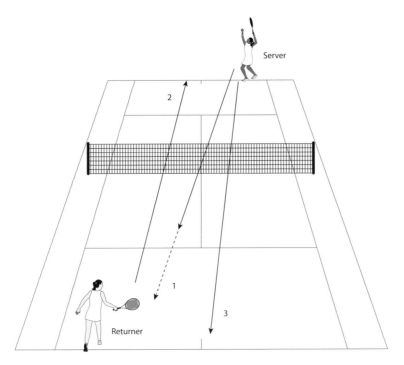

Objective: To develop serve and return consistency.

Equipment: Players, court, rackets and balls.

Description: Players play against each other ideally on the full court (although the drill also works crosscourt if there are more players). Players play points against each other, but before they can play the point to win they have to work together to achieve a rally of serve – return – ball 3. Once ball 3 has been played then the players play the point to win. If this rally of three is not achieved then no point is scored and the players try again until the rally is achieved. Every three points the players should swap roles so that both have a turn at serving and returning.

Coaching points: The main focus for the server in this drill should be recovering quickly after the serve so that they can be in a good position to hit ball 3 since mistakes are often made on this shot due to poor footwork. The returner should concentrate on consistency on the return. Meeting the ball in front of their body and aiming it back down the middle of the court is the best way to achieve this.

Progression: Progress this drill by asking the server to hit ball 3 to the opposite side of the court to the one served to. This way they are starting to develop a serve and groundstroke pattern to move the returner out of position.

drill 61 3 serves per point

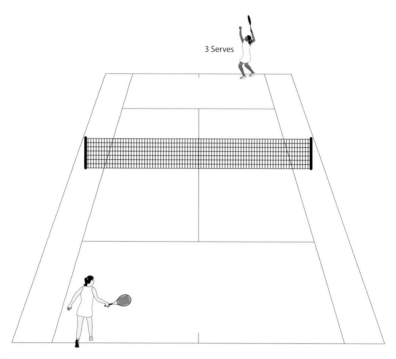

3 Serves

Objective: To allow players valuable serving practice within a competitive play situation.

Equipment: Players, court, rackets and balls.

Description: Players play singles points as normal, but the server is allowed three serves per point instead of two. This effectively means that the server has two attempts to hit a first serve, allowing for an immediate correction of the fault if the serve is missed. This is an invaluable drill since it allows players to practise their serve while still maintaining their focus on competing.

Coaching points: Ensure players try to hit another first serve if they miss the first one (since players often forget they have an extra serve), and encourage them to try to hit to the same place again (even if their opponent knows where they are trying to serve to). This ability to self-correct quickly is vital for tennis players.

Progression: As competence develops, allow players only three extra serves per game – and allow them to use them whenever they choose. Therefore, they could take an extra serve if they hit a double fault, or they could choose to hit another first serve that they missed first time around. This progression forces them to plan their serves more carefully.

drill 62 1 serve per point

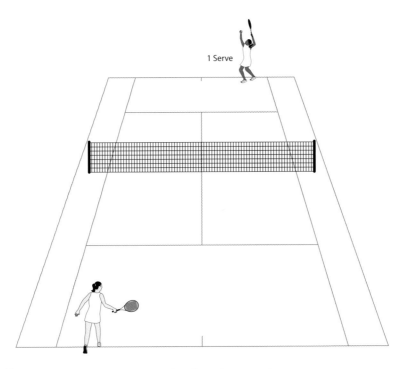

1 Serve

Objective: To improve the quality of a player's second serve.

Equipment: Players, court, rackets and balls.

Description: Players play singles points as normal, but the server is only allowed one serve per point instead of two. This is an excellent drill to help improve the quality of a player's second serve, and it also highlights the importance of having a second serve that an opponent finds difficult to attack.

Coaching points: Encourage players to hit their second serve positively and with commitment. This can be done by awarding the returner only one point for a service error but two points if they hit a winning return. This encourages the server to hit a more aggressive serve to prevent the returner from attacking too easily.

drill 63 serving patterns

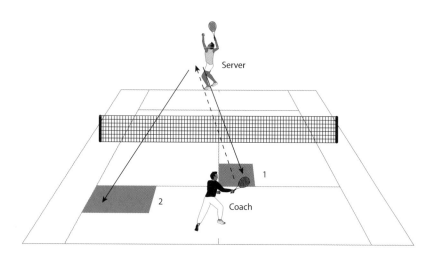

Objective: To help players construct patterns of play based around their serve.

Equipment: Players with rackets and balls to serve with, plus a coach with a basket of balls.

Description: The server hits a serve and a second shot to pre-determined areas of the court. This drill allows the server to develop specific patterns of play based around the serve. The player and coach agree where the serve and groundstroke are to be hit to. After the player hits the serve, the coach then feeds a second ball (simulating a return of serve) for the player to hit his/her second shot with. Repeat this two-ball sequence to a variety of serve and second shot targets.

Coaching points: It is important for the coach to try to feed the return of serve as realistically as possible. This means timing the feed well (i.e. feeding the return just as the serve is crossing the baseline), and feeding from the most realistic court position (e.g. the coach should feed from a wide position if the serve is hit wide). Encourage players to split-step after serving to maintain balance and to try to play their second shot from inside the baseline if working on an aggressive pattern of play.

Progression: Vary the serve and second shot targets and look for players to hit their second shots with both forehands and backhands. Develop first serve patterns where the server tries to dominate, and second serve patterns where the server tries to at least neutralise the returner's dominance. As competence increases, play the point out competitively after the serve and second shot have been hit.

drill 64 reaction returns

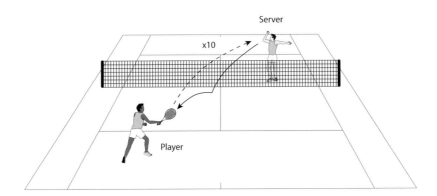

Server

x10

Player

Objective: To help players return a strong first serve by improving reaction speed and returning technique.

Equipment: Players, court, rackets and balls.

Description: The player is positioned halfway between the service line and the baseline in one half of the court with the server standing at the net diagonally across from them. The server throws a ball overarm, down into the service box for the player to try to return. Repeat this 10 times before switching roles.

Coaching points: Encourage an alert ready position and look for a short and simple swing to help the returner contact the ball in front of their body. Their technique needs to be simple and compact since they have very little time to prepare for the shot. Begin the drill with the server throwing to the same place each time before varying the throw as the return develops.

Progression: As competence increases, ask the server to hit normal serves instead of throwing the ball, but keep the returner positioned halfway between the service line and the net. Again, encourage short and simple swings with the returner trying to use the pace of the oncoming serve to return with rather than trying to generate pace themselves.

drill 65 percentage returns

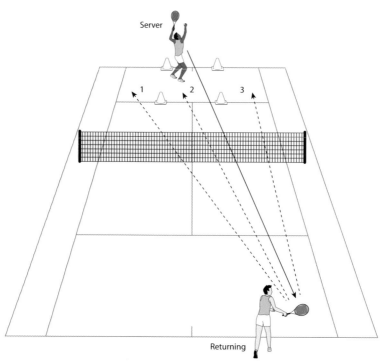

Objective: To develop tactical awareness and sound technique for the return of serve.

Equipment: Players, court, rackets, balls and marker cones.

Description: Using the cones mark the server's end of the court so that it is split into three channels. The server then serves to the returner, the returner practises the return but the players do not play the point out. The returner chooses which of the three channels to return to based on the serve that they receive.

Coaching points: Help players understand which return targets offer the best combination of consistency and effectiveness. If they receive a very good serve then the centre channel is the best option since it gives the most margin for error. If the serve is slightly weaker then encourage the 'across the body' return – this is where a serve to the forehand is directed across to the right-handed server's forehand, and a serve to the backhand across to the server's backhand.

Progression: Once players have gained an understanding of the principle of percentage returns then allow them to play the point out. However, the returner is awarded a bonus point if their return hits the correct target area.

drill 66 neutralise with the return

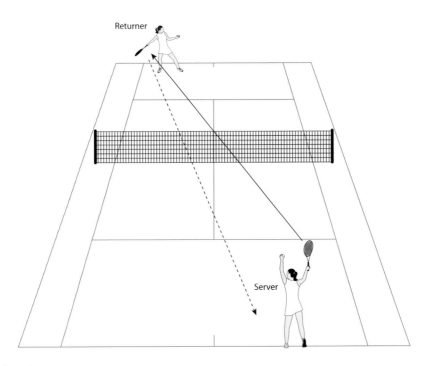

Objective: To develop a return of serve that neutralises the threat of a strong serve.

Equipment: Players, court, rackets and balls.

Description: Players play points as normal but the point is worth three if the return is hit into the court beyond the service line. It is important to note that the point is worth three to either player (not just the returner) so players need to concentrate immediately!

Coaching points: This is an excellent drill to encourage depth on the return, which is often the best way to neutralise a strong serve. Encourage players to hit their returns deep into court even if they sometimes hit the ball beyond the baseline. Remember, a player could make two return errors in a row before hitting a really effective return, yet they would still be ahead in the score.

Progression: As the quality of the return develops, only allow the point to be played out if the return is hit beyond the service line. The point is still worth three when the return is hit beyond the service line but any short returns lose the point immediately. Alternatively, ask the server to shout 'yes' if they feel the return has neutralised well enough. The point is only played out on the 'yes' returns and is worth one point to both players. Asking the server to judge the quality of the return gives vital feedback to the returner – something rarely given by an opponent.

drill 67 return attack

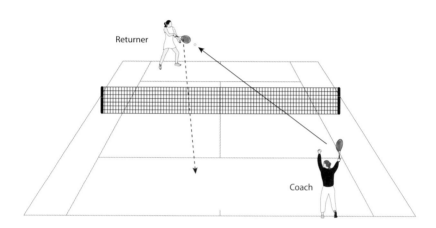

Returner

Coach

Objective To help players construct attacking patterns of play based around their return.

Equipment: Players with rackets and a coach with a basket of balls.

Description: The player hits a return and a second shot to pre-determined areas of the court. This drill allows the player to develop specific patterns of play based around their return. The player and coach agree where the return and next groundstroke are to be hit to. After the coach serves and the player hits the return, the coach then feeds a second ball for the player to hit his/her second shot with. Repeat this two-ball sequence to a variety of return and second shot targets.

Coaching points: It is important for the coach to try to feed the shot after the return as realistically as possible. This means timing the feed well (i.e. feeding the ball just as the return is crossing the baseline), and feeding from the most realistic court position (e.g. the coach should feed from a wide position if the return is hit wide). Encourage players to split-step just as the coach serves and to try to play their second shot from inside the baseline if working on an aggressive pattern of play.

Progression: Vary the return and second shot targets and look for players to hit their second shots with both forehands and backhands. Develop second serve return patterns where the returner tries to dominate, and first serve return patterns where the returner tries to at least neutralise the server's dominance. As competence increases, play the point out competitively after the return and second shot have been hit.

DOUBLES

The Williams sisters have never been ranked No. 1 in doubles, however when they do team up their record is outstanding.

drill 68 throw and catch doubles

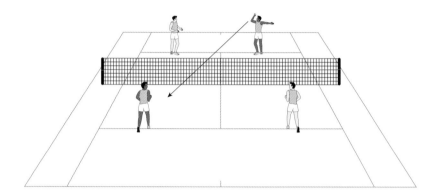

Objective: To develop spatial awareness and movement as a team in doubles.

Equipment: Players, court and balls.

Description: The players work in teams of two. One team plays against another team with all four players starting on the service line. One of the players starts the point off with an overarm throw crosscourt into the diagonal service box. The players then play the point out against each other, catching the ball after one bounce and sending it back with an underarm throw. For younger players it is best not to use the tramlines, but older and more experienced players should include them since there is more space to work with.

Coaching points: To move well as a team in doubles the players need to know and do two things:

- They need to adjust their position quickly as the ball is going away from them so that they are in a good position by the time the ball comes towards them
- Where they recover to depends on where they threw the ball to. For example, if they throw the ball wide to one side of the court then one of the players must stay wide on the other side of the court to cover an angled reply

Progression: Introduce a rule that allows players to go forwards and catch the ball before it bounces. If they do this, they are then allowed to throw the ball overarm and be more aggressive – giving them a great chance to win the point.

drill 69 coach fed scenarios

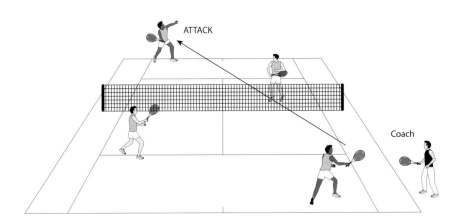

Objective: To allow a doubles pair to experience a range of tactical situations within one drill.

Equipment: Players, court, rackets and coach with a basket of balls.

Description: Two pairs take a one up/one back doubles position on the court with the coach positioned at one end to the side of the court. The pair at the opposite end to the coach can request the tactical situation they will play the point from by calling 'attack' or 'defend'. If the call is 'attack' then the coach feeds a relatively easy ball for them to attack with. If the call is 'defend' then the coach feeds a more difficult ball for them to deal with. The point is played out from this position and after 10 points have been played the pairs change ends and switch roles.

Coaching points: Make sure that both players in the pair get a chance to play the point out as often as possible by mixing the type of ball given when attacking and defending. For example, making the pair defend may mean feeding the ball as a lob over the net player's head, and allowing them to attack may mean feeding a floating ball for the net player to intercept with. Encourage the pair to communicate well and to coordinate their movement whenever possible. Also, make sure they receive roughly the same amount of easy feeds and difficult feeds.

drill 70 waves

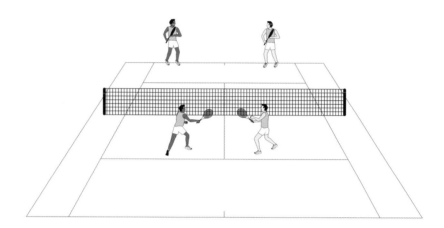

Objective: A fun team game that develops teamwork and good net play.

Equipment: Players, court, rackets and balls.

Description: Players work in teams of two or three. One team plays against another and all the players start off spread out across the baseline. One player starts the point off with an underarm serve and the players play the point out. The team that wins the point then moves forwards to the service line and starts the next point from there. If that team were to win that point then they would move forwards to the net, but if they were to lose it then they would drop back and the winning team would move forwards.

The teams carry on playing, moving up and back each time a point is won and lost. If one of the teams makes it to the net and then wins the point from the net then they win a game, and both teams return to the baseline to start again.

Coaching points: Using the lob is perhaps the most important tactic in this game. Help players to lob more effectively by explaining how a lob over their opponent's backhand side is often the most effective, and how lobbing when the opposing team is very close to the net increases the space that can be used behind them. Help players deal with being lobbed by training them to spot it coming by reading the racket face position of the baseline player.

drill 71 singles to doubles

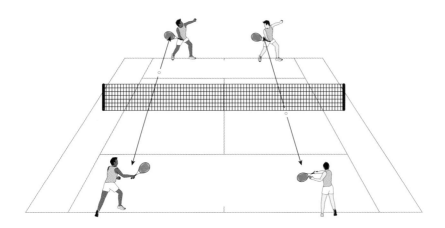

Objective: To develop concentration, communication and teamwork.

Equipment: Players, court, rackets and balls.

Description: Two players rally from the baseline to each other in half a court with another two players doing the same thing in the other half court. The players work cooperatively and try to reach as high a rally count as possible. However, as soon as one of the rallies on the court breaks down, the other rally becomes a competitive doubles point. This means that all four players play the point out and the players on the same baseline become doubles partners! When this rally finishes, the players go back to rallying in pairs until the next doubles opportunity.

Coaching points: Encourage players to keep an eye on their partner's rally while also maintaining their concentration on their own rally. It is really important for the doubles partners to communicate well – particularly at the start of the doubles point. Look for players to try to move in to the net together as quickly as possible when the doubles rally starts. This aggressive movement will often prove successful.

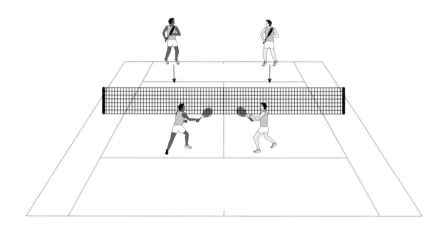

Objective: To help players understand how to beat an opposing pair who are at the net.

Equipment: Players, court, rackets and balls.

Description: The players work in teams of two. Opposing teams play against each other in the full doubles court. The pairs take it in turns to be the net players who start from the net with an underarm feed. Every five points the pairs switch roles. The net pair tries to win with volleys and smashes and the baseline pair tries to win with lobs and passing shots. If either pair wins in this way then they win one point. However, if the baseline pair manages to get inside the service line and win the point then they win three points instead of one. This is known as 'stealing the net'!

Coaching points: The baseline pair needs to put the net pair under pressure by using a combination of dipping shots to their feet and lobs over their heads. Whenever the net pair is put under pressure it is vital that the baseline pair move up together as fast as possible to try to volley the next shot for a winner.

drill 73 doubles champions

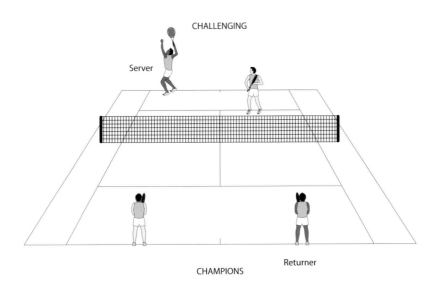

CHALLENGING

Server

Returner

CHAMPIONS

Objective: A fun way to play doubles with more than four players per court.

Equipment: Players, court, rackets and balls.

Description: Players work in teams of two. Arrange the pairs so that there are three or four pairs per court depending on numbers in the group. One of the pairs starts as the champion pair; they go to one end of the court and both play at the baseline. The other pairs are the challengers; they take it in turns to come on and play two points against the champion pair. They serve one point from the right and the other point from the left court. The first challenging pair to win four points become the champions, and the champions become challengers. When there is a new champion pair the other challenging pairs keep any points that they have – this ensures that eventually everybody gets a turn as the champion pair. The challengers must alternate the server each time they come in for their two points.

Coaching points: In between points the coach should remind the serving pair about the importance of good positioning. The server should stand on the baseline about halfway between the centre of the court and the inside tramline and their partner should be in the centre of the service box. These positions put the serving team in the best position to cover, and hopefully take advantage of, any return of serve.

Progression: Introduce conditions that allow a pair to become the champions automatically. Choose the condition depending on what the players need to practise. For example, players could become champions straight away if they win with an intercept volley.

drill 74 intercept the feed

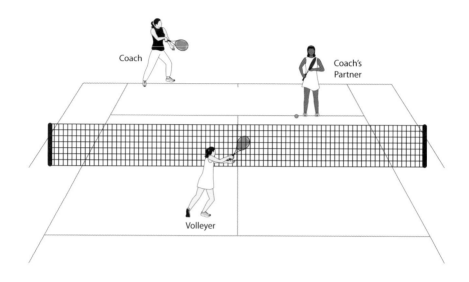

Objective: To develop the effectiveness of the intercept volley in doubles.

Equipment: Players, court, rackets and balls.

Description: The coach feeds crosscourt from a returning position. The volleyer (standing opposite the coach at the net) moves across the court and volleys the ball down to the feet of Player B who is standing on the service line as the coach's partner. The point is played out from this position. Play points to five before switching roles.

Coaching points: Make sure Player A moves forwards to the intercept volley as well as across the court. Ask them to try to play down to the feet or just behind the heels of Player B. Look for Player A to contact the ball in front of their body with a firm wrist. Encourage Player B to move backwards or forwards depending upon the quality of the intercept volley (i.e. an aggressive intercept volley will require Player B to move back to defend it and vice versa).

Progression: The coach should start to vary the feed by sometimes hitting down the line or hitting a lob to prevent Player A from moving across too early. Vary the difficulty of the feed to allow Player B the chance to attack as well as defend against the intercept volley.

drill 75 intercept the rally

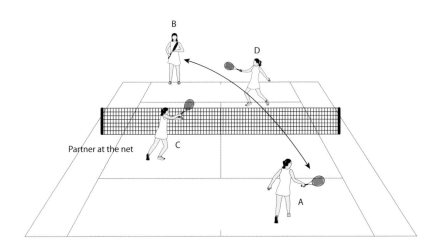

Objective: To develop the effectiveness of the intercept volley in a rally situation.

Equipment: Players, court, rackets and balls.

Description: Two doubles pairs take up a one-up/one-back doubles formation. Player A rallies crosscourt from the baseline to Player B. They are only allowed to rally crosscourt. Players C and D try to intercept their respective opponent's groundstroke by moving across the net and volleying down to the feet of their opponent at the net. Play the point out once the intercept volley has been played. Play points to five before switching roles.

Coaching points: Make sure Players C and D move forwards to the intercept volley as well as across the court. Ask them to try to play down to the feet or just behind the heels of the opposing net player. Encourage them to take some risks by anticipating early since the opposing baseline player can only hit crosscourt. Look for the opposing net player to move quickly to defend (or attack) against the intercept volley.

Progression: The baseline players must rally two balls crosscourt each, but then they are allowed to hit down the line (and also use the lob) to play the point out. Encourage smart decision making as to when to hit down the line. Look for the net players to try to maintain an aggressive mentality when intercepting at the net.

drill 76 1st volley drill

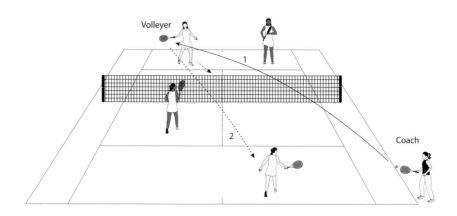

Objective: To develop the first volley when approaching the net in doubles.

Equipment: Players with rackets and coach with a basket of balls.

Description: Two doubles pairs take up a one-up/one-back doubles formation. Player A moves forwards from the baseline to join his/her partner at the net. As Player A crosses the service line the coach feeds a groundstroke from the opposite baseline (from behind the baseline player). Player A must volley this ball back to the baseline player beyond the service line. The point is played out between the two pairs from here. Play points to five before switching roles.

Coaching points: Make sure Player A tries to direct their first volley away from the opposing net player and beyond the service line. Encourage the volleying team to move forwards together, and look for the opposing net player to try to intercept Player A's first volley if it is not hit well enough.

Progression: Instead of the coach feeding a groundstroke, the doubles pairs play points with serves. The baseline player of either pair must try to approach the net as quickly as possible. If they win a point by playing a deep first volley they win two points instead of one. The server wins three points instead of one if they choose to serve and volley, and manage to play a deep first volley.

drill 77 two up two back

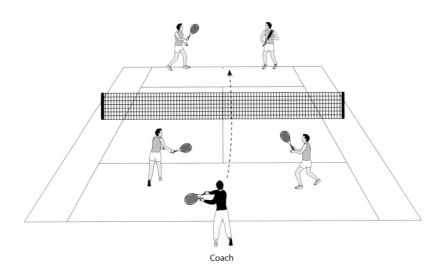

Coach

Objective: To develop a doubles pair's ability to take the net away from their opponents.

Equipment: Players, court, rackets and balls.

Description: One doubles pair is positioned together at the net, while their opponents both start on the baseline. The coach feeds a ball in from behind the net pair to the baseline pair and the point is played out from here. The objective of the drill is for the baseline pair to find a way of approaching the net and for the net pair to defend against this. Play points to seven before switching roles.

Coaching points: Encourage the baseline pair to experiment with different ways of approaching the net. These include chipping the ball to the feet of the net pair, using the lob, and hitting down the line or aggressively down the middle of the court. Look for both pairs to communicate well and for them to move as a team up and back from the net. The coach should also vary the type of feed given to the baseline pair – allowing them to use a number of different first shots to start the rally.

drill 78 four up

Coach

Objective: To develop fast hand skills and the ability to hold a net position under pressure.

Equipment: Players, court, rackets and balls.

Description: Two doubles pairs take up a net position on the service line opposite each other. The coach feeds a ball in from behind one of the pairs and the point is played out in full. All four players must start on the service line as the ball is fed in from the coach, although they can move in once the point starts. Play points to seven before the pairs change ends and play again.

Coaching points: This is a quick-fire drill requiring fast reaction speed since the ball is volleyed very quickly between players. Encourage players to stand their ground and maintain a contact point in front of their body since there will be very little time to swing the racket. Look for each pair to stay close together, not allowing a big space to open up between them. Lob volleys can be hit although they should be played with caution since a short lob volley can be a dangerous option!

Coach

Objective: To encourage positive net play as a doubles pair.

Equipment: Players, court, rackets and balls.

Description: Two doubles pairs take up a baseline position on opposite sides of the court. The coach feeds a ball in from behind one of the pairs and the point is played out in full. Both pairs try to find a way to the net during the point. If a pair wins a point at the net they win three points instead of one. Play points to 11 before the pairs change ends and play again.

Coaching points: Encourage the players to move up to the net together as a pair. This is important since big gaps will appear between them if their movement is not coordinated well enough. Players need to communicate strongly and make smart decisions as to when to approach the net. Look for the approaching pair to play down the middle of the court often to reduce the angles available to their opponents. The coach should vary the types of feed given to encourage creativity and variety of shot.

drill 80 rotating doubles

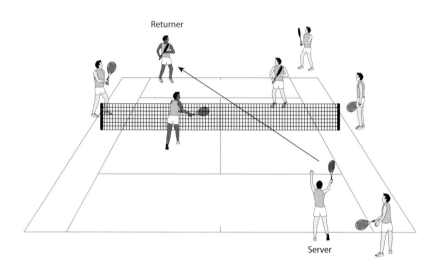

Objective: To play doubles points when there are more than four players per court.

Equipment: Players, court, rackets and balls.

Description: Four players are set up to play a doubles point with one of the ends designated as the serving end. The remaining players are positioned at various waiting stations. The stations can vary depending on how many extra players there are: one player can be at each net post, one player waiting behind the server, one player can be at the back of each end, etc.

The four players play two points with the same player serving once from the right court and once from the left. After two points have been played the players all rotate one place clockwise. Some players move into the waiting stations and the players in those stations move into the next playing position, etc. Whichever player has moved into the designated serving position serves for the next two points. The players count their own individual scores adding one point every time they are part of a winning team.

Coaching points: The receiver's partner often starts the point in the incorrect position during this drill. The correct position for the receiver's partner to start the point is around the service line. This puts them in position to try and cover a volley from the server's partner off the return of serve. If the return goes crosscourt and back to the server then the receiver's partner can close in on the net and look for an attacking volley of their own.

drill 81 one bounce doubles

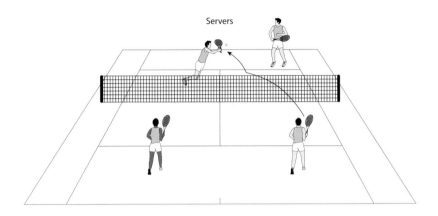

Objective: A higher level doubles game to encourage attacking net play.

Equipment: Players, court, rackets and balls.

Description: The players play doubles points using normal scoring. The condition is that the serving team is only allowed to let the ball bounce once on their side of the court. If the ball bounces for a second time on their side of the net during the point then they lose the point automatically.

Coaching points: The serving pair needs to get to the net as quickly as possible. The best way to do this is for the server to use the serve and volley tactic. When serving and volleying the server should follow their serve with three or four strong strides towards the net before balancing for their volley at around the same time as the receiver returns the serve.

Progression: Progress to no bounces allowed for the servers. Also, encourage the returning pair to attack the net by enforcing the one bounce rule on their side of the court (meaning that only the oncoming serve is allowed to bounce).

drill 82 serve and volley doubles

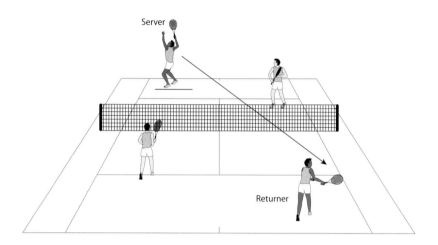

Objective: To help players experience and improve the serve and volley tactic in doubles.

Equipment: Players, court, rackets, balls and one court line.

Description: Players pair up and play doubles points against another pair. They score points as normal except that the serving team must use the serve and volley tactic on both first and second serves. This means that the server must follow their serve in to the net in order to volley the opponent's return. Allow less experienced players to start serving on a line midway between the baseline and the service line. This will mean they reach the net more quickly. Move the line towards the baseline as competency increases.

Coaching points: Encourage the server to move in to the net using two or three quick strides after serving. It is really important that they also use a small split-step as the returner is about to hit the return. Look for the server's partner at the net to also start moving forwards, so that any weak return can be pounced on aggressively (since the volleyer's body weight is already moving towards the ball). It may be that the server's first serve is much more effective than their second serve – in this case allow the second serve to be hit from closer in than the first.

GAME SCENARIOS

Sabine Lisicki of Germany plays an open stance backhand return.

drill 83 think of a tactic

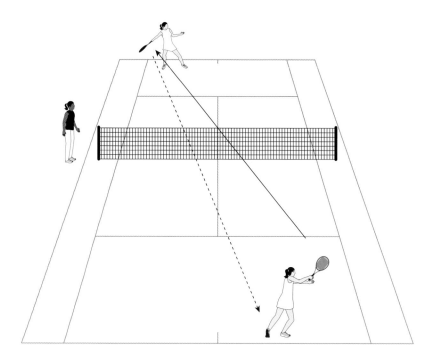

Objective: A fun yet highly competitive game that encourages the use of a variety of tactics.

Equipment: Players, court, rackets and balls.

Description: Set the players up in points play, ideally in the full court if space and numbers allow. The coach chooses a particular tactic, but does not tell the players what it is. The players have to play points against each other while the coach watches. The first player to win a point using the tactic that the coach was thinking of wins the game. The coach then chooses a different tactic and the game starts again.

Coaching points: Encourage the players to keep trying different tactics until they get to the one that the coach was thinking of. If the players are struggling then the coach can give them a clue (e.g. which area of the game the tactic relates to, etc). If the players are still struggling then the coach can tell the players what the tactic is – it is then up to the players to try to win the point using that tactic.

drill 84 win 3 for 3

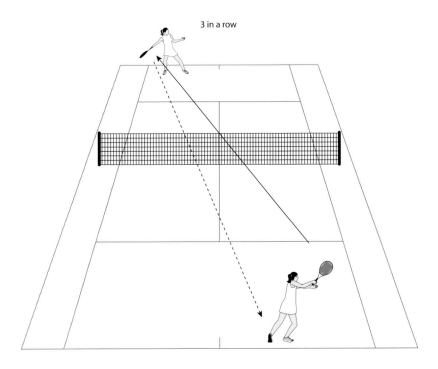

3 in a row

Objective: A competitive game that helps improve concentration and consistency.

Equipment: Players, court, rackets and balls.

Description: In a competitive singles match it is very common for both players to win a very similar number of points. However, the winner of the match is usually the player who wins the most sequences of points. In this drill the players play points in a full court, although if there is limited space then the drill still works with players using a half court. The players play and score points as normal, however, if a player wins three points in a row they win a bonus of three points to add to their score. The players play first to 11 or 21 points depending on the time available.

Coaching points: The key to this drill is to maintain concentration and to carry on playing positive tennis for three points in a row. It is easy to lose concentration or to get defensive once the first two points have been won and there is a chance of a three point bonus. Teach the players to stay focused on 'how' they are going to play the current point – rather than being distracted by the outcome of the point they are about to play. A good way to do this is to use a key teaching point to focus on during competitive play – such as 'contact the ball in front' or 'accelerate the racket head'.

drill 85 dominate with the forehand

Objective: A competitive game that helps develop strategic thinking.

Equipment: Players, court, rackets and balls.

Description: The players play singles points in a full court. Depending on the numbers of players there may be a need to rotate the players in and out. As the players play they have to try and use their forehand as much as possible to attack their opponent. The first player to hit two forehands in a row during the point is then playing for three points instead of one, while the point is only worth one point to the opposing player.

Coaching points: This drill is great for developing players' awareness of how the ball they hit to their opponent affects the kind of ball that they receive back. Encourage the players to think about how, when they attack with their first forehand, they can start to predict their opponent's reply and adjust their position to give them an opportunity to hit the second forehand. For example, an aggressive forehand hit into the opponent's backhand will usually produce a weaker crosscourt reply. So the player can start to move across to their backhand side to give them a better chance of using the forehand for their second shot.

drill 86 find the backhand

Objective: A competitive game that helps players to attack their opponent's backhand.

Equipment: Players, court, rackets and balls.

Description: Players play points in the full singles court. They have to try to attack their opponent's backhand during the point. The first player who manages to make their opponent play three backhands during the rally is then playing for three points instead of one, while the point is only worth one point to the opposing player. The three backhands do not have to be in a row – it is simply three in total.

Coaching points: The most important shots in this drill are the crosscourt backhand and the down the line forehand since these are the shots that will most often be used to find the opponent's backhand. Develop the quality of the players' crosscourt backhand by encouraging them to angle the ball so that it crosses the sideline before the baseline on their opponent's side of the court. On the forehand down the line, make sure that players remember that they will be hitting over the high part of the net; so even though they will be attacking they need to maintain good height on this shot.

drill 87 singles champions

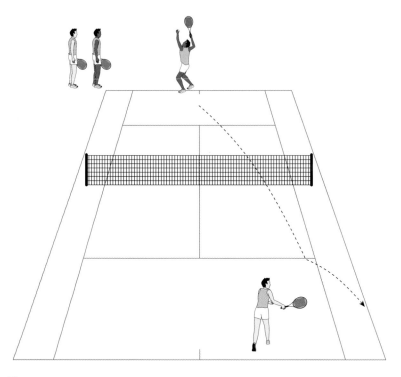

Objective: A fun way to get more than two players per court playing singles matches.

Equipment: Players, court, rackets and balls.

Description: One player starts as the champion. Depending on the number of players another two, three or possibly four players take it in turns to play against the champion for two points at a time. Each challenging player keeps their own game score against the champion. The first challenging player to win a game against the champion becomes the new champion. At that point the champion joins the challenger – but is always the last player in against the new champion.

Coaching points: The rotational format of this game is ideal for working with players in match play situations. As the players drop out emphasise to them what they did well in the previous points and then agree what they are going to try and do better next time they go in to play. These gaps in play provide great coaching opportunities.

drill 88 pick a card

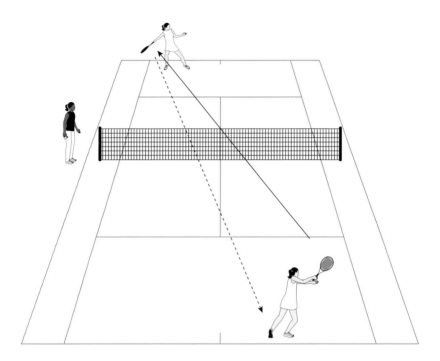

Objective: To raise awareness of the different types of game styles and character traits in tennis.

Equipment: Players with rackets and balls, coach with style cards.

Description: Each player chooses a card before playing singles points. On the card there is a description of a certain type of game style (e.g. serve and volleyer, defensive baseliner, aggressive all-court player, etc) or a certain type of character (e.g. bad temper, dubious line caller, ultra positive player, etc). The player has to try to play according to the game style/character described on the card. Their opponent has to guess which game style/character they are attempting to play.

Coaching points: Encourage players to have fun exaggerating their roles fully so they truly experience a different way of playing and feeling on court. Coaches should note which type of game style suits each player the most and should get feedback from the player as to how each one felt. Exaggerating certain characteristics will also help players become more aware of their own character traits as a player – and which ones help or hurt their performance.

drill 89 collect your thoughts

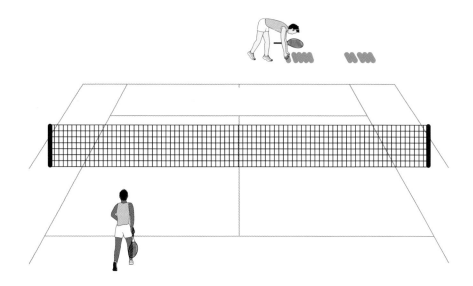

Objective: A drill to raise awareness of positive and negative self-talk during competitive play.

Equipment: Players, court, rackets, balls, 20 clothes pegs per pair.

Description: Players play singles points in either the full court or half court (depending upon numbers). At the start of play the players put two piles of five pegs each at the back of their court (well behind the baseline so they don't get in the way). One pile represents positive self-talk and the other represents negative self-talk. After each point the player moves one peg from one pile to the other depending upon their thoughts after the point. For example, if the player plays the point and has a positive thought, a peg from the negative pile is put into the positive pile and vice versa. The points are stopped when the player has collected all 10 pegs in one of the piles!

Coaching points: This is a great drill to raise a player's awareness of how they think between points. The benefit of using pegs is that it allows the coach to 'see' the nature of their players' thoughts. It is important for the players to understand that they can play well and still lose – so their thoughts should reflect their performance rather than just the result of each point. This is something that should be reinforced by the coach whenever possible.

drill 90 hang your peg

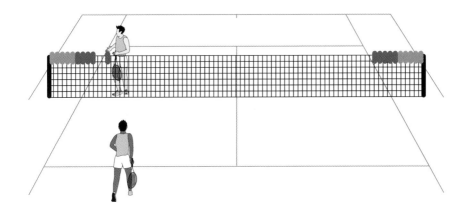

Objective: To help players assess their performance more objectively.

Equipment: Players, court, rackets, balls, 20 clothes pegs per pair (two different colours).

Description: Players play singles points in either the full court or half court (depending upon numbers). At the start of play the players clip 10 pegs to the top of the net above their right hand tramline. There should be five pegs of one colour and five pegs of another colour (e.g. red and blue). The red pegs represent their opponent's good play and the blue pegs represent their own poor play. The player who loses the point has to take one peg and clip it further inside the net – based on their assessment of the point. For example, if the losing player hits an unforced error they should choose a blue peg, however, if their opponent hits a forehand winner they should choose a red peg instead.

Coaching points: This drill allows a player to start differentiating between their own performance and the outcome of the point. This is important because less experienced players will often only use the result to gain confidence. However, in tennis, it is common for a player to play well and lose or to play poorly and win. In either situation it is important for players to look beyond the result by assessing how they performed in a more objective way. The pegs allow the coach to 'see' how their player viewed their performance and this will provoke important debate between player and coach.

FUN GAMES

Andy Murray chases back from the net in an attempt to stop the ball from getting past him.

drill 91 human skittles

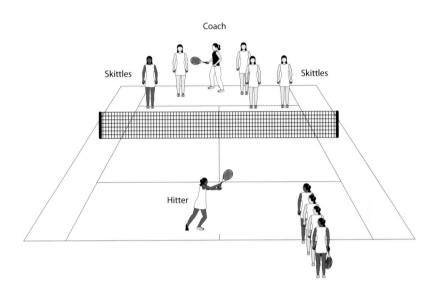

Objective: A fun game that's great for lots of players on one court.

Equipment: Players, court, rackets and balls.

Description: Split the players into two even teams. One team are the 'skittles' – they spread themselves around the coach's end of the court and stand upright. The other team are the 'hitters' – they line up on the other side of the court ready to come in and hit the ball. As each hitter comes in for their turn the coach feeds a ball to either their forehand or backhand. The player hits the ball and if they hit a skittle then that player (the skittle) sits down. The coach counts how many hits are required to knock all the skittles down at which point the teams swap over. The winning team is the one that required the fewest hits.

Coaching points: Players coming in for their turn need to remember that the ball can be fed to either their forehand or backhand, so they need to be waiting in an alert ready position. Make sure the feed is deep enough so that the hitter is a long way from any skittles who may be standing close to the net!

drill 92 3-touch tennis

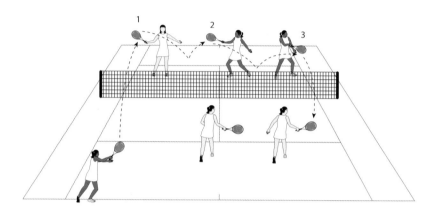

Objective: A fun team game for developing racket head control.

Equipment: Players, court, rackets and balls.

Description: Split the players into two even teams. The two teams spread out on opposing sides of the court, each player with a racket. One player starts the point off with an underarm serve and the teams play the point out against each other. However, they are not allowed to hit the ball straight back over the net; the ball has to be hit by three different team members before it goes over the net on the third hit. The ball is allowed to bounce once in between each hit. Once the point is finished a different player starts the next point.

Coaching points: To play this game effectively the players need to be able to 'cushion' the ball with their racket – this takes the pace off the ball and will help control it for the next team member to hit.

Progression: Make the game more challenging by only allowing the ball to bounce once per side.

drill 93 one racket rallies

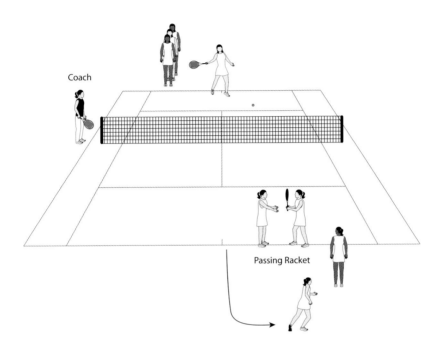

Coach

Passing Racket

Objective: A fun team game that develops consistency and movement.

Equipment: Players, court, balls and one racket per team.

Description: Split the players into two even teams. Each team lines up on opposing sides of the court behind the baseline, with the first player in the line holding the racket. One of the players (or the coach) starts the point with an underarm serve and the point is played. After each shot the player that hits has to pass the racket to the next player in the line and then move to the back of the queue, the player receiving the racket then moves to play the next shot. Every time the rally breaks down the coach feeds the ball in to start the next point.

Coaching points: Encourage the players to think tactically in this game. If they can get the opposing player a long way wide or forwards then that player has further to move to pass the racket to the next player!

Progression: Each point can be started with an overarm serve and bonus points awarded for winning volleys, since going to the net is very difficult in this game.

drill 94 prisoners

Coach

Prison

Objective: A fun team game ideal for lots of players on a court.

Equipment: Players, court, rackets and balls.

Description: Split the players into two even teams. The two teams spread out on opposing sides of the net, each player with a racket. The coach feeds the ball in from the side of the court and the teams then play the point to win with the player best positioned for each shot aiming to hit it back over the net.

When the point finishes the coach decides which member of the losing team was responsible for losing the point – that player then drops out into the 'prison' area at the side of the court. When a team that has a player in prison wins a point they can choose to either release the longest serving prisoner from their team or send another member of the opposing team to prison!

The winning team is the team that manages to get all of the opposing team into prison first. At this point all the players are released back onto the court and the game starts again.

Coaching points: The coach must ensure that it is not always the same players that go to prison first. The player who missed the shot doesn't have to be the one to leave the court, since it may be that another player played a poor shot earlier in the rally and this player could be chosen as the new prisoner.

drill 95 tennis cricket

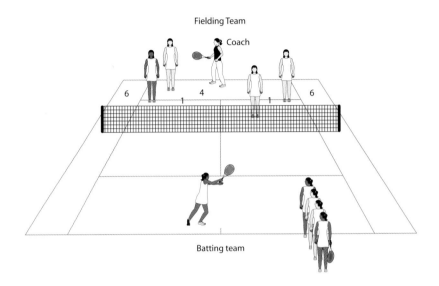

Fielding Team

Coach

6   4   6

1   1

Batting team

Objective: A fun game that involves lots of players on one court.

Equipment: Players, court, rackets and balls.

Description: Split the players into two even teams. One team spreads out around the court at one end – this is the 'fielding' team. The other team lines up one behind the other with a racket each at the other end of the court – this is the 'batting' team. The batting team come in one at a time; the coach feeds each player either a forehand or a backhand from the other side of the court. The batting player hits their shot and tries to get it to bounce on the other side of the court, the fielding team try to catch the ball before it bounces.

If the ball is hit out, in the net, or is caught then the hitting team lose a wicket. If the ball bounces on the court then the hitting team score runs. If it lands in the service box one run is scored, if it lands beyond the service line four runs are scored, and if the ball lands between the tramlines six runs are scored. Once five wickets fall the batting team are all out and the teams swap over.

Coaching points: The fielding team need to think about how to organise themselves to best cover the court, and the batting players need to decide whether to go for the more difficult shots for more runs or the easier shots for just the one run!

drill 96 run around lives

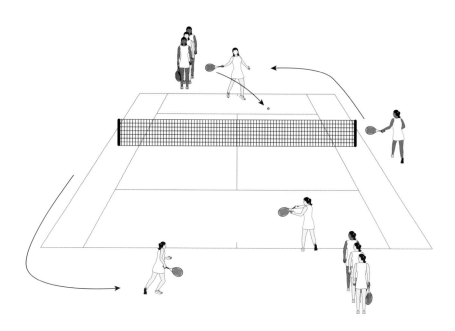

Objective: A fun and active game that develops consistency and movement.

Equipment: Players, court, rackets and balls.

Description: The players start in two lines – one at either end of the court. Players stand one behind the other behind the baseline with a racket each. The first player in the line (or the coach) starts the rally with an underarm serve. The rally is then maintained with each player taking it in turns to come in, hit their shot, and then run around to join the queue at the other end of the court.

If a player makes a mistake or has a winning shot hit past them they lose a life. If a player loses three lives then they drop out of the game. Once all the players are out apart from the last two then those two players play against each other in a one point 'winner takes all' final.

Coaching points: Safety is important since players can be running fast around the court. Make sure that all the players run the same way around the court to avoid collisions. Also ensure that there are no obstacles on the side of the court or around the net posts that players could trip over.

drill 97 team tennis

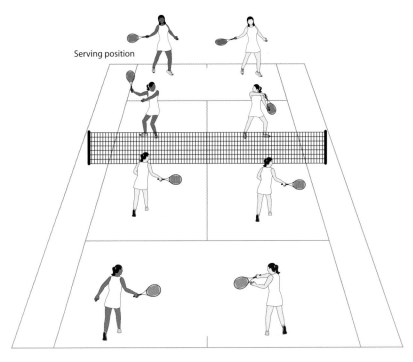

Serving position

Objective: A game to develop strategy and an understanding of court position.

Equipment: Players, court, rackets and balls.

Description: Two teams of three or four players each play points against the other in the doubles court. Each team can decide what formation they want to play and can change this formation at any time. For example, a team could decide to position two players at the net and two at the baseline then change to all four players at the baseline, etc. An overarm serve is used to start the point and this must be allowed to bounce in the service box as normal. Every player must have a turn at serving and returning at some point during the game. Play points to 11 before changing ends and repeating.

Coaching points: This is a great game to help players to think about how they play best. Encourage players to take up positions that allow them to play their favourite shots most often. Look for good communication within the team and lots of strategic thinking!

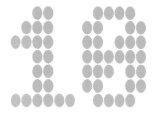

COOLING DOWN

The USA's Venus Williams tries to stay cool mentally and physically at the change of ends.

drill 98 racket twist and stretch

Objective: To improve flexibility and to cool the body down.

Equipment: Players and rackets.

Description: The players work in pairs with a racket between each pair. The pair finds a space and stands back-to-back about one metre apart. One player starts with the racket. The players start by passing the racket to each other in a figure of eight movement around their body and behind their back. After 10 passes they change the direction of the racket. The players move on to passing the racket between their legs and then back over their head – again they change the direction of the racket after 10 passes.

Coaching points: Make sure the players use slow and smooth movements; the emphasis must be on the quality of their movement rather than their speed.

drill 99 hamstring reach

Objective: To stretch the hamstrings as part of a cool down.

Equipment: Players on court.

Description: The players start on one side of the court and stretch out face down on the floor. They then slowly start to walk their feet up to their hands, but keeping their legs as straight as possible and their palms flat on the floor. Once they've got their feet close to their hands they start to walk their hands away from their feet until they are lying on the floor again. At this point they repeat the exercise.

Coaching points: Slow and smooth movements are important and the full stretch position with hands and feet close together should be held for around 20 seconds.

drill 100 jog across – stretch back

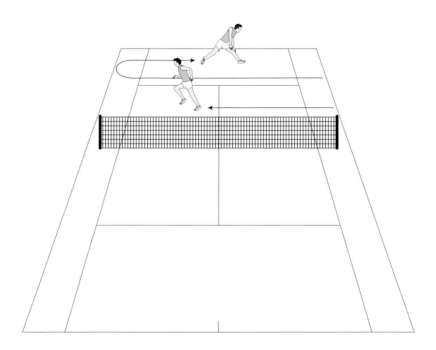

Objective: To cool the body down.

Equipment: Players on court.

Description: The players spread out along the outside tramline of the court. The players jog across the court slowly, making sure that they keep their arms loose and relaxed. On the way back the players stretch one of the muscle groups – concentrating on smooth movements and holding the stretches. The players then repeat the process but the coach (or a player) calls out a different stretch for the way back.

Coaching points: Players should hold each stretch for around 20 seconds and should concentrate on keeping loose and relaxed. Emphasise the quality of each movement rather than the speed of movement across the court.

drill 101 tennis bowls

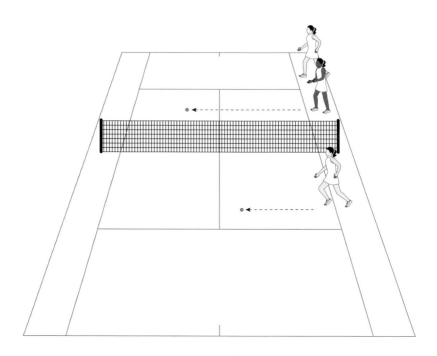

Objective: A game to calm the energy levels of a group at the end of an active session.

Equipment: Players, court and balls.

Description: The players find a space in one of the tramlines of the court – each player with a ball. The players have to roll the ball across the court and attempt to stop the ball in the tramline on the other side of the court. If they are successful then they score a point. They then try again from the other tramline; the players compete to see who can score the most points before the end of the session.

Coaching points: The players should use their knees to get low to the ground to help them roll accurately and smoothly. Encourage them to transfer their weight with balance onto their front foot as they step forwards and roll the ball (since this mirrors a forehand groundstroke technique). Look for the ball to roll across the court rather than bounce, and for the players to 'hold' their finish position for a second or two before standing up.